Strategic Cost Analysis
The Evolution from Managerial to Strategic Accounting

Strategic Cost Analysis
The Evolution from Managerial to Strategic Accounting

John K. Shank

Vijay Govindarajan

*both of
Amos Tuck School of
Business Administration
Dartmouth College*

1989

Homewood, IL 60430
Boston, MA 02116

Sponsoring editor: Ron M. Regis
Project editor: Ethel Shiell
Production manager: Ann Cassady
Compositor: Compset, Inc.
Typeface: 10/12 Times Roman
Printer: Arcata Graphics/Kingsport

Library of Congress Cataloging-in-Publication Data

Shank, John K.
    Strategic cost analysis : the evolution from managerial to
strategic accounting/John K. Shank, Vijay Govindarajan.
        p.   cm.
    Bibliography: p.
    Includes index.
    ISBN 0-256-07042-3
    1. Cost accounting. 2. Managerial accounting. I. Govindarajan,
Vijay. II. Title. III. Title: Strategic accounting.
HF5686.C8S458   1989
658.1'511—dc19   88–36882
                                                             CIP

Printed in the United States of America

    6 7 8 9 0 K 6 5 4 3 2 1

We dedicate this book to the women in our lives:
Diane
Kirthi, Tarunya, and Tapasya

Contents

Introduction

This book represents a new emphasis in managerial accounting. It is based on the premise that managerial accounting must explicitly consider strategic issues and concerns. We believe that the incorporation of strategic concerns into cost analysis represents a very natural, overdue extension of managerial accounting which itself only became popular about 30 years ago (Anthony 1956; Horngren 1962).

Historically, managerial accounting replaced cost accounting as a framework for decision making by demonstrating that the cost accounting framework lacked decision relevance. The cost accounting framework of the 1940s failed to take into account the decision analytic framework that had become popular in the 1950s. In the past decade, there has been a dramatic extension of decision analysis to take explicit account of strategic issues. During the past 15 years, several books (Henderson 1979; Porter 1980) and dozens of articles (e.g., Buzzell et al. 1975; Hambrick 1981; Snow and Hrebiniak 1975) have been published in the field of strategic management. In addition, two new journals (*Strategic Management Journal* and *Journal of Business Strategy*) have been introduced in the strategy area during the past 10 years. Also, traditional management journals such as *Administrative Science Quarterly, Academy of Management Journal,* and *Academy of Management Review* have, during the past decade, started to regularly publish articles on strategic analysis. It is now time for management thinking about cost analysis to move forward again and to incorporate this newly enriched decision analysis paradigm. Strategic accounting will supplant managerial accounting as a framework for supporting decision making by demonstrating that managerial accounting lacks strategic relevance. The major purpose of this book is to encourage managerial accountants and accounting educators to begin actively presenting cost analysis in the broader strategic context.

The timing of this book couldn't have been better. During the past year, several academics as well as practitioners have highlighted the serious shortcomings of the prevailing costing systems in American corporations and have asserted that management accounting is part of the problem in American industry today rather than part of the solution:

Corporate management accounting systems are inadequate for today's environment. In this time of rapid technological change, vigorous global and domestic competition, and enormously expanding information processing capabilities, management accounting systems are not providing useful, timely information for the process control, product costing, and performance evaluation activities of managers.

Johnson and Kaplan, 1987

Most large companies seem to recognize that their cost systems are not responsive to today's competitive environment . . . the methods they use to allocate costs among their many products are hopelessly obsolete. . . . Quite simply, accurate cost information can give a company a competitive advantage. . . .

Worthy, *Fortune*, 1987

Cost-accounting is wrecking American business. If we're going to remain competitive, we've got to change (our costing systems).

Pryor, *Business Week*, 1988

One message comes through overwhelmingly in our experiences with the three firms, and with the many others we talked and worked with. Almost all product-related decisions—introduction, pricing, and discontinuance—are long term. Management accounting thinking (and teaching) during the past half-century has concentrated on information for making short-run incremental decisions based on variable, incremental, or relevant costs. It has missed the most important aspect of product decisions.

Cooper and Kaplan, *Management Accounting*, 1988

Recently, the American Accounting Association and the National Association of Accountants jointly sponsored a special symposium on "Cost Accounting, Robotics, and the New Manufacturing Environment" which dealt principally with the pitfalls of management accounting as practiced and taught today (Carpettini and Clancy 1987).

Our book responds to these harsh criticisms of the current cost accounting systems by providing a new framework, *strategic cost analysis,* which adapts the traditional body of knowledge called cost analysis to the rapidly developing body of knowledge on strategy formulation and implementation.

STRATEGIC COST ANALYSIS: AN OVERVIEW

Cost analysis is traditionally viewed as the process of assessing the financial impact of managerial decision alternatives. How is strategic cost analysis different? It is cost analysis in a broader context, where the *stra-*

tegic elements become more conscious, explicit, and formal. Here, cost data is used to develop superior strategies en route to gaining sustainable competitive advantage. No doubt, cost accounting systems can help in other areas as well (inventory valuation, short-term operating decisions, etc.). However, the use of cost data in strategic planning has not received the attention it deserves, either in cost accounting textbooks or in management practice. There is a billion dollar a year market in strategic cost analysis consulting services dominated by such firms as Bain & Company, Boston Consulting Group, Booz Allen & Hamilton Inc., McKinsey & Company, and Monitor Inc. Yet, not one business school in the country teaches a course built around the specific techniques used by these firms in this business niche. A sophisticated understanding of the firm's cost structure can go a long way in the search for sustainable competitive advantage. This is what we refer to as "strategic cost analysis."

Consistent with this perspective, the central theme of the book is that accounting exists within a business primarily to facilitate the development and implementation of business strategy. Under this view, business management is a continuously cycling process of (1) formulating strategies, (2) communicating those strategies throughout the organization, (3) developing and carrying out tactics to implement the strategies, and (4) developing and implementing controls to monitor the success of the implementation steps and hence the success in meeting the strategic objectives. Accounting information plays a role at each of the four stages of this cycle:

- **At stage one,** accounting information is the basis for financial analysis, which is one aspect of the process of evaluating strategic alternatives. Strategies which are not financially feasible or which do not yield adequate financial returns cannot be appropriate strategies.

- **At stage two,** accounting reports constitute one of the important ways that strategy gets communicated throughout an organization. The things we report are the things people will pay attention to. Good accounting reports are thus reports which focus attention on those factors which are critical to success of the strategy adopted.

- **At stage three,** specific tactics must be developed in support of the overall strategy and then carried through to completion. Financial analysis, based on accounting information, is one of the key elements in deciding which tactical programs are most likely to be effective in helping a firm to meet its strategic objectives.

- **And finally, at stage four,** monitoring the performance of managers or of business units usually hinges partly on accounting information. The role of standard costs, expense budgets, and annual profit plans in providing one basis for performance evaluation is well accepted in businesses all around the world. These tools must be explicitly adapted to the strategic context of the firm if they are to be maximally useful.

Three important generalizations emerge from this way of viewing management accounting:

- Accounting is not an end in itself, but only a means to help achieve business success. There is thus no such thing as good accounting practice or bad accounting practice, per se. Accounting techniques or systems must be judged in light of their impact on business success.

- Specific accounting techniques or systems must be considered in terms of the roles they are intended to play. A concept such as return on investment analysis may have little relevance for assessing the performance of middle level managers in situations where investment decisions are made centrally. However, this concept may at the same time be critically important in assessing the attractiveness of different strategic investment options. Accounting analysis which is terrible for some purposes may be great for others. A working knowledge of management accounting thus involves knowledge of the multiplicity of roles accounting information can play.

- In evaluating the overall accounting system for a business, mutual consistency among the various elements is critical. The key question is whether the overall "fit" with strategy is appropriate. For example, a standard cost system with tight, engineered cost allowances may be an excellent tool for assessing manufacturing performance in a business following a strategy of being the low cost producer. However, developing such an accounting tool might well be a waste of time in a business pursuing a strategy of new product innovation and "skimming."

Summarizing these three generalizations, the key management questions to ask about any accounting idea are listed below.

- Does it serve an identifiable business objective? (facilitate strategy formulation, . . . assess managerial performance . . .)
- For the objective it is designed to serve, will the accounting idea enhance the chances of attaining the objective?
- Does the objective whose attainment is facilitated by the accounting idea fit strategically with the overall thrust of the business?

For an accounting idea to be useful for a particular purpose in a particular business at a particular time, all three of these questions must yield an affirmative answer. This book is about accounting as a tool for strategic management. The ideas presented here are intended to be ones which do yield affirmative answers to these three questions with explicit attention to the strategic issues involved.

ORGANIZATION OF THE BOOK

The book is organized around eight chapters. Each chapter typically contains a real-world business situation and an analysis of that situation using cost data. While the solutions are situation-specific, they can be effectively used to develop the strategic cost analysis framework. The chapters deal with four major themes in strategic cost analysis:

- Chapters 1 and 2 deal with new ways of thinking about integrating old familiar cost concepts such as fixed versus variable costs, contribution analysis, and cost-volume-profit relationships.
- Chapters 3, 4, and 5 deal with some new cost analysis concepts not yet in the textbooks such as value chain analysis and "activity" costing.
- Chapters 6 and 7 deal with differentiated controls for differentiated strategies—tieing accounting controls explicitly to strategy.
- Chapter 8 identifies certain major strategic business decisions where formal financial analysis cannot be of any help—thus the subtitle, strategic financial analysis which isn't.

We have provided below a brief synopsis of each chapter.

In Chapter 1, we present a short case (dealing with a private label opportunity for a bicycle manufacturer) which we believe will support a "strategic" analysis as well as a "relevant cost" analysis. The chapter demonstrates that strategic cost analysis is often just a different application of the same sorts of financial tools we normally use today. But, even when the analysis is different only in its focus and not in its underlying structure (such as a value chain analysis), the insights can differ dramatically. What we are emphasizing is a need for managers to be aware that cost analysis must explicitly consider strategic issues and concerns.

Chapter 2 presents a case where contribution analysis suggests a low-price, high-volume marketing approach. Use of the full cost metric and explicit consideration of strategic positioning point out the pitfalls of the penetration pricing approach and suggest the higher price as the more viable and attractive option. The purpose of this chapter is to highlight the pitfalls of marginal contribution information as the basis for so-called short-run decision making.

Chapter 3 uses the "famous" Crown Cork & Seal Company case to address the following set of interrelated issues: What is strategic value chain analysis? Why is it important? How does it differ from traditional cost analysis? What modifications need to be made to the traditional cost accounting systems to facilitate value chain analysis?

Chapter 4 uses a simplified case to demonstrate how "traditional" and even "modern" approaches to product costing can be dramatically deceiving about product profitability. The hero is a concept called "activity costing" which we will contrast with the villain—costing based on thruput or output volumes (volume-based costing, for short).

Chapter 5 describes the application of "transactions-based" overhead allocation concepts in a specialty paper mill. The existing mill-level cost accounting system—typical of those in the paper industry—assigns overheads to products based on tons produced. As we will demonstrate, the conventional system is subject to the same fundamental flaw which plagues any output volume-based allocation system when applied to a complex product line encompassing high-volume and low-volume products. Namely, the system averages away important cost differences among products by failing to charge particular products for the costs which result from transactions or activities which are caused by those particular products. When the high level of handling and processing activities associated with products that are processed in small batches are averaged across the entire product line, *high*-volume products are *overcosted* by a *small* amount but *low*-volume products are *undercosted* by a *large* amount (per unit). This distortion in product costs, in many cases, encourages firms to choose inappropriate strategies. Low-volume specialty products appear to be significantly more profitable than they actually are, tempting firms to emphasize—incorrectly—the low-volume business. This problem is widespread in American industry, yet it is virtually ignored in cost accounting books.

Chapter 6 presents a short disguised case to emphasize how variance analysis—an important tool of performance evaluation—becomes most meaningful when it is tied explicitly to the strategic context of the business under evaluation.

Chapter 7 presents a live (but disguised) case to illustrate two key ideas in strategically based cost analysis and control: (1) The use of cost analysis to identify the differing strategic positions of three products of a large chemicals manufacturer and (2) the use of differentiated management controls focusing on the differing key success factors for the differentiated strategies for the three products.

In Chapter 8 we present a case study which concerns the timberland holdings of a major paper and wood products company. Whether to retain a very large investment (6.8 million acres) or divest part or even all of it is the subject of the case. This is certainly a major strategic decision for the firm since it involves *billion dollar* cash flows spread out over 30- to 50-year growth cycles. The case study emphasizes two points. First, it illustrates very nicely how the role of financial analysis shrinks dramatically when the strategic issues become this major. As this case illustrates, for problems of this duration and magnitude, financial analysis tends not to be very strategically oriented and strategic analysis tends not to be very financially oriented. Second, the case illustrates how the choice of internal accounting and reporting systems can play a major role in shaping the way firms look at the strategic issues. The accounting reports definitely constitute a "lens" through which management views the current results of its past strategic commitments. When that lens most closely resembles a pair of "rose colored glasses," the strategic assessment process is affected in ways management may not fully appreciate.

The primary audiences for this book are managers concerned about meaningful cost analysis, accounting educators, and accounting students. Our hope is that what is taught and learned in the accounting classrooms should fit the real world of today. We have successfully used the contents of this book in the required Management Accounting course in the First Year of the Tuck MBA program. We could also recommend its use in an elective course on Strategic Cost Analysis for Second Year MBA students. Instructors could assign each chapter for a single class session and use the assignment questions at the end of the chapter to structure and guide the class discussion.

REFERENCES

Andrews, K. R. *The Concept of Corporate Strategy*. Homewood, Ill.: Dow Jones-Irwin, 1971.

Anthony, R. N. *Accounting*. Homewood, Ill.: Richard D. Irwin, 1956.

Buzzell, R. D., G. Bradley, and R. G. M. Sultan. "Market Share—A Key to Profitability." *Harvard Business Review* 53, January–February 1975, pp. 97–106.

Carpettini, R., and D. K. Clancy (eds). *Cost Accounting, Robotics, and the New Manufacturing Environment*. Sarasota, Fla.: American Accounting Association, 1987.

Cooper, R., and R. S. Kaplan. "How Cost Accounting Distorts Product Costs." *Management Accounting,* April 1988, pp. 20–27.

Hambrick, D. C. "Environment, Strategy, and Power within the Top Management Team." *Administrative Science Quarterly* 26, 1981, pp. 253–76.

Henderson, B. D. *Henderson on Corporate Strategy*. Cambridge, Mass.: Abt Books, 1979.

Horngren, C. T. *Cost Accounting: A Managerial Emphasis*. Englewood Cliffs, N.J.: Prentice-Hall, 1962.

Johnson, T. H., and R. S. Kaplan. *Relevance Lost: The Rise and Fall of Management Accounting*. Boston, Mass.: Harvard Business School Press, 1987.

Kelly, K. "That Old-time Accounting Isn't Good Enough Anymore." *Business Week,* June 6, 1988, p. 112.

Porter, M. E. *Competititve Strategy.* New York: The Free Press, 1980.

Snow, C. C., and L. G. Hrebiniak. "Strategy, Distinctive Competence, and Organizational Performance." *Administrative Science Quarterly* 20, 1975, pp. 546–58.

Worthy, F. S. "Accounting Bores You? Wake Up." *Fortune,* October 12, 1987.

PART ONE

New Applications of Familiar Cost Concepts

CHAPTER 1

Making Strategy Explicit in Cost Analysis: The Baldwin Bicycle Case Study*

In this chapter we present a short case (dealing with a private label opportunity for a bicycle manufacturer) which we believe will support a "strategic" analysis as well as a "relevant cost" analysis. The chapter demonstrates that strategic cost analysis is often just a different application of the same sorts of financial tools we normally use today. But, even when the analysis is different only in its focus and not in its underlying structure (such as a value chain analysis), the insights can differ dramatically. What we are emphasizing is a need for managers to be aware that cost analysis must explicitly consider strategic issues and concerns. We believe this represents a very natural extension of the managerial accounting framework which itself only became popular about 30 years ago (Anthony 1956; Horngren 1962). Managerial accounting replaced cost accounting as a framework for financial analysis for decision making by demonstrating that the cost accounting framework lacked decision relevance. The cost accounting framework failed to take into account the advances in decision analysis which had become popular in the 1950s. In the past decade there has been another dramatic extension of decision analysis to take explicit account of strategic issues.[1] It is now time for management thinking about cost analysis to move forward again to incorporate this newly enriched decision analysis paradigm. Strategic account-

---

*A modified version of this chapter appeared in *Sloan Management Review,* Spring 1988. Reprinted with permission.

[1]During the past 15 years, several books (e.g., Andrews 1971; Henderson 1979; Porter 1980) as well as articles (e.g., Buzzell et al. 1975; Hambrick 1981; Snow and Hrebiniak 1975) have been published in the field of strategic management. In addition, two new journals (*Strategic Management Journal* and *Journal of Business Strategy*) have been introduced in the strategy area during the past 10 years. Also, traditional management journals such as *Administrative Science Quarterly, Academy of Management Journal,* and *Academy of Management Review* have, during the past decade, started to regularly publish articles on strategic analysis.

ing will supplant managerial accounting as a framework for decision making by demonstrating that managerial accounting lacks strategic relevance.

THE BALDWIN BICYCLE COMPANY CASE

In May 1983, Suzanne Leister, marketing vice president of Baldwin Bicycle Company, was mulling over the discussion she had had the previous day with Karl Knott, a buyer from Hi-Valu Stores, Inc. Hi-Valu operated a chain of discount department stores in the Northwest. Hi-Valu's sales volume had grown to the extent that it was beginning to add "house-brand" (also called "private-label") merchandise to the product lines of several of its departments. Mr. Knott, Hi-Valu's buyer for sporting goods, had approached Ms. Leister about the possibility of Baldwin's producing bicycles for Hi-Valu. The bicycles would bear the name "Challenger," which Hi-Valu planned to use for all of its house-brand sporting goods.

Baldwin had been making bicycles for almost 40 years. In 1983, the company's line included 10 models, ranging from a small beginner's model with training wheels to a deluxe 12-speed adult's model. Sales were currently at an annual rate of about $10 million. The company's 1982 financial statements appear in Exhibit 1. Most of Baldwin's sales were through independently owned retailers (toy stores, hardware stores, sporting goods stores) and bicycle shops. Baldwin had never before distributed its products through department store chains of any type. Ms. Leister felt that Baldwin bicycles had the image of being above average in quality and price, but not a "top-of-the-line" product.

Hi-Valu's proposal to Baldwin had features that made it quite different from Baldwin's normal way of doing business. First, it was very important to Hi-Valu to have ready access to a large inventory of bicycles, because Hi-Valu had had great difficulty in predicting bicycle sales, both by store and by month. Hi-Valu wanted to carry these inventories in its regional warehouses, but did not want title on a bicycle to pass from Baldwin to Hi-Valu until the bicycle was shipped from one of its regional warehouses to a specific Hi-Valu store. At that point, Hi-Valu would regard the bicycle as having been purchased from Baldwin, and would pay for it within 30 days. However, Hi-Valu would agree to take title to any bicycle that had been in one of its warehouses for four months, again paying for

SOURCE: R. N. Anthony and J. S. Reece, *Accounting: Text and Cases* (Homewood, Ill.: Richard D. Irwin, 1983), pp. 742–44.

EXHIBIT 1   Financial Statements (thousands of dollars)

BALDWIN BICYCLE COMPANY
Balance Sheet
As of December 31, 1982

Assets		Liabilities and Owners' Equity	
Cash	$ 342	Accounts payable	$ 512
Accounts receivable........	1,359	Accrued expenses..........	340
Inventories................	2,756	Short-term bank loans......	2,626
Plant and equipment (net) ..	3,635	Long-term note payable	1,512
		Total liabilities.......	4,990
		Owners' equity............	3,102
	$8,092		$8,092

Income Statement
For the Year Ended December 31, 1982

Sales revenues	$10,872
Cost of sales..........................	8,045
Gross margin	2,827
Selling and administrative expenses	2,354
Income before taxes	473
Income tax expense....................	218
Net income	$ 255

it within 30 days. Mr. Knott estimated that on average, a bike would remain in a Hi-Valu regional warehouse for two months.

Second, Hi-Valu wanted to sell its Challenger bicycles at lower prices than the name-brand bicycles it carried, and yet still earn approximately the same dollar gross margin on each bicycle sold—the rationale being that Challenger bike sales would take away from the sales of the name-brand bikes. Thus, Hi-Valu wanted to purchase bikes from Baldwin at lower prices than the wholesale prices of comparable bikes sold through Baldwin's usual channels.

Finally, Hi-Valu wanted the Challenger bike to be somewhat different in appearance from Baldwin's other bikes. While the frame and mechanical components could be the same as used on current Baldwin models, the fenders, seats, and handlebars would need to be somewhat different, and the tires would have to have the name *Challenger* molded into their sidewalls. Also, the bicycles would have to be packed in boxes printed with the Hi-Valu and Challenger names. These requirements were expected by Ms. Leister to increase Baldwin's purchasing, inventorying, and production costs over and above the added costs that would be incurred for a comparable increase in volume for Baldwin's regular products.

On the positive side, Ms. Leister was acutely aware that the bicycle boom had flattened out, and this plus a poor economy had caused Baldwin's sales volume to fall the past two years.* As a result, Baldwin currently was operating its plant at about 75 percent of one-shift capacity. Thus, the added volume from Hi-Valu's purchases could possibly be very attractive. If agreement could be reached on prices, Hi-Valu would sign a contract guaranteeing to Baldwin that Hi-Valu would buy its house-brand bicycles only from Baldwin for a three-year period. The contract would then be automatically extended on a year-to-year basis, unless one party gave the other at least three-months' notice that it did not wish to extend the contract.

Suzanne Leister realized she needed to do some preliminary financial analysis of this proposal before having any further discussions with Karl Knott. She had written on a pad the information she had gathered to use in her initial analysis; this information is shown in Exhibit 2.

---

*Note: The American bicycle industry had become very volatile in recent years. From 1967 through 1970 sales average about 7 million units a year. By 1973 the total was up to a record 15 million units. By 1975 volume was back down to 7.5 million units. By 1982 volume was back up to 10 million units, still well below the peak years.

EXHIBIT 2   Data Pertinent to Hi-Valu Proposal (*Notes taken by Suzanne Leister*)

---

1. *Estimated first-year costs of producing Challenger bicycles* (average unit costs, assuming a constant mix of models):

Materials	$39.80*
Labor.................................	19.60
Overhead (@ 125% of labor)	24.50†
	$83.90

2. *Unit price and annual volume:* Hi-Valu estimates it will need 25,000 bikes a year and proposes to pay us (based on the assumed mix of models) an average of $92.29 per bike for the first year. Contract to contain an inflation escalation clause such that price will increase in proportion to inflation-caused increases in costs shown in item 1, above; thus, the $92.29 and $83.90 figures are, in effect, "constant-dollar" amounts. Knott intimated that there was very little, if any, negotiating leeway in the $92.29 proposed initial price.

3. *Asset-related costs* (annual variable costs, as percent of dollar value of assets):

Pretax cost of funds (to finance receivables or inventories)	18.0%
Recordkeeping costs (for receivables or inventories).............	1.0
Inventory insurance...	0.3
State property tax on inventory	0.7

EXHIBIT 2 *(concluded)*

Inventory-handling labor and equipment........................   3.0
Pilferage, obsolescence, breakage, etc. 0.5

4. *Assumptions for Challenger-related added inventories* (average over the
  year):
    Materials: two month's supply.
    Work in process: 1,000 bikes, half completed (but all materials for them
        issued).
    Finished goods: 500 bikes (awaiting next carload lot shipment to a Hi-
        Valu warehouse).

5. *Impact on our regular sales:* Some customers comparison shop for bikes,
  and many of them are likely to recognize a Challenger bike as a good value
  when compared with a similar bike (either ours or a competitor's) at a higher
  price in a nonchain toy or bicycle store. In 1982, we sold 98,791 bikes. My
  best guess is that our sales over the next three years will be about 100,000
  bikes a year if we forego the Hi-Valu deal. If we accept it, I think we'll lose
  about 3,000 units of our regular sales volume a year, since our retail
  distribution is quite strong in Hi-Valu's market regions. These estimates do
  not include the possibility that a few of our current dealers might drop our
  line if they find out we're making bikes for Hi-Valu.

Note: The information about overhead in item 1 of case Exhibit 2 can be used to infer
that fixed manufacturing overhead is about $1.5 million per year.
*Includes items specific to models for Hi-Valu, not used in our standard models.
†Accountant says about 40 percent of total production overhead cost is variable; 125
percent of DL$ rate is based on volume of 100,000 bicycles per year.

This short but very rich case is particularly useful for illustrating
"strategic accounting" because the conclusions which emerge from a
"relevant cost" analysis diverge so widely from the conclusions suggested
by a "strategic cost" analysis. In order to contrast the two perspectives,
we will first present the relevant cost analysis—an exercise in financial
analysis for a potential "extra chunk" of business.

RELEVANT COST ANALYSIS OF THE HI-VALU OFFER

This perspective would typically consider cost behavior as a starting
point. From case facts, it is not difficult to deduce that the incremental
cost of producing a Challenger bike is about $69 (material, direct labor,
and about $9+ of variable overhead). The idea here is to back out the
allocated share of fixed manufacturing overhead from the unit cost. In
terms of the management decision, the point is that a $92+ selling price
provides much more incremental profit than the standard cost of $84+
might suggest. Since the fixed costs are already being covered by the regular business, they need not be covered again.

A second element of the relevant cost analysis would typically be the cost of carrying the incremental investment needed to support the incremental sales. This calculation has two components—the incremental working capital investment (no incremental fixed assets are required) and the annual carrying charge percentage. The extra investment can fairly readily be estimated as follows:

Raw material (2 months stock)
   ~ 4,000 bikes × ~ $40 =   ~ $160,000

Work in process (1,000 units)
   "½ finished" implies about $55 semi-finished cost (100%
   of material plus ½ of labor and variable overhead)
   ~ 1000 bikes × ~ $55 =   ~   55,000

Finished units in our factory
   ~ 500 bikes × ~ $69 =   ~   35,000

Finished units in the HV warehouse
   per case "facts," about 2 months supply, on average
   ~ 4,000 bikes × ~ $69 =   ~   280,000
   (The range here is probably from
   ~ $100,000 to ~ $550,000)

   Accounts receivable (30 days sales)
   ~ 2,000 bikes × ~ $92 =   ~   185,000

(Less a trade credit offset)
   Assume 45 days credit from the materials suppliers
   ~ 3,000 bikes × ~ $40 =   (~   120,000)

   Net Extra Investment
   (range = ~$400,000 to ~$900,000)   ~ $595,000

The major judgment in this calculation is the number of bikes in the consignment inventory. We will not try to formalize that uncertainty any more carefully here because the issue is not really central to the point of this paper. Choosing the annual carrying charge rate is, however, clearly a major element in the analysis. There are several basic ideas involved here:

- Capital is not free.
- The relevant charge is the "cost of capital" *plus* incremental carrying costs (insurance, handling, taxes . . .).
- Cost of capital is some form of weighted average across the debt and equity capital sources used by the firm.

- Any specific number chosen is, at best, a rough approximation because the "true cost of capital" cannot be observed.
- If incremental debt costs 18 percent, before tax, a first cut weighted average cost of capital (after tax) might be 13 percent assuming ⅓ debt and ⅔ equity in the capital structure [⅓ × (18% × .5) + ⅔(15%)].
- Incremental carrying cost seems to be about 4 percent a year (before tax) for inventory and 0 percent for receivables, rejecting part of the case note as being just an allocation of common costs.
- Combining carrying costs and cost of capital, an after-tax charge of 15 percent for inventory and 13 percent for receivables is a reasonable first-cut.

Combining these two components of the carrying cost calculation produces an annual cost number somewhere between about $56,000 (for a $400,000 investment) and about $131,000 (for a $900,000 investment). A mid-range estimate is about $100,000 or $4 per bike (over the estimated 25,000 Challenger bikes). The range here is from about $2 per bike to about $5 per bike. This is well below the $11.50 after-tax marginal contribution [($92 − $69) × .5], even at the high end of the investment and carry cost range.

A third element of the relevant cost analysis would typically be an "erosion" or "cannibalization" charge for the lost sales of regular Baldwin bikes as a direct result of Hi-Valu's entry into the market. The two main judgments here are how much the charge should be, assuming it is relevant, and whether, in fact, this is a relevant charge against the project. If a charge is to be assessed, it should be the lost profit contribution from the lost sales. It is possible to calculate that the regular business yields a contribution of about $44 per bike [sales price of ~$110 ($10.8M/$99K) less variable cost of ~$66 ($8M − 1.5M*/$99K)]. Thus, if 3,000 units are lost, the impact on profit would be about $130,000 (3,000 × ~$44). Partly offsetting this, the incremental working capital investment (calculated earlier) would decline somewhat.

Whether or not an erosion charge is relevant is arguable. Assuming that 3,000 customers who otherwise would have bought a Baldwin bicycle do in fact buy a Challenger bicycle, the lost profit is certainly *real* to Baldwin. On the other hand, it probably is reasonable to assume that HV will find someone to make Challenger bikes, and that Baldwin's sales will drop somewhat as a result, regardless of what Baldwin does. Thus, the sales are lost once HV enters the market, regardless of Baldwin's actions. Baldwin's base volume has become 96,000 units instead of 99,000 and the erosion charge is not incremental to the Challenger deal. The marketing dimension of a relevant cost analysis supports the idea that one cannot stop new products from eroding the sales of old products. A firm can only choose to sell the new products or not to sell them. In this context, focusing on the erosion is not only arrogant (our products are impervious to decline unless we cannibalize them), but also short-sighted (we lose the opportunity to sell new products but sales of the old products decline *anyway*). Thus, a strong argument can be made to exclude the erosion charge.

Summarizing the components of the cost analysis, we can calculate the incremental profitability as follows:

1. Incremental profit contribution for 25,000 bikes = ~$288,000, after tax.
    [($92 − $69) × 25,000 × .5]
2. The incremental capital charge would be about $100,000, after tax.
3. Incremental residual income after tax is about $188,000 per year on a $600,000 investment.
    This is a very attractive return!

This is clearly only a first approximation of the incremental return because it ignores the time value of money. A multiperiod, discounted cash flow approach would be preferable. Also, it leaves open the time period for the project. However, refining this calculation does not change the basic message that the HV deal is very attractive from a short-run, incremental financial analysis perspective.

If there are caveats in the analysis, they center around the following issues.

- The consigned inventory issue: Do we really have to tolerate this sort of imposition on normal business terms by HV?

- The capacity issue: Is it wise to tie up most of our excess capacity, unused though it *currently* is, for several years at well below normal prices?

- The long-run/short-run cost issue: Is it really appropriate to ignore fixed overhead in a project which uses almost 20 percent of our capacity over a three-year period?

- The uncertainty of HV demand issue: What happens to the incremental analysis if HV actually takes fewer than 25,000 bikes or more than 25,000?

- The incremental debt capacity issue: Can we borrow an incremental $400,000 to $900,000 to finance the project?

Only the last one of these five potential concerns requires additional analysis. The other four are more qualitative than quantitative. The debt capacity issue does require explicit attention.

The $2.6 million level of short-term debt is very high for a year-end balance sheet for a company like Baldwin. December 31 should be a point in the year of nearly maximum liquidity for a manufacturer of a seasonal, consumer durable product like bicycles. Production for the Christmas season should be shipped and paid for by now, and the production buildup for spring should not be started yet. One clue to this liquidity crunch is the high level of inventory still on hand at this slack time of year. The $2.7M of inventory represents about 120 days supply ($2.7/8.0 × 365) at a time of the year when very little stock should be on hand. Much of this inventory is likely to be "slow-moving" or even obsolete product. And, it is all financed with short-term debt!

Even though the incremental residual income from the project looks very attractive, it is problematic whether the firm could justify borrowing yet another $600,000 or so for the HV project. One imaginative thought in this regard is reworking some of these bikes as Challenger bikes. This approach would save much of the material cost per bike. It also substitutes rework labor for new assembly labor. If the idea is feasible, it probably involves an incremental cost of much less than $69 per bike, which then cuts down the financing need. Our experience with the case indicates that managers who get this far in the analysis are sufficiently attracted by the high incremental profit to lead them to argue that the financing problem would not be insurmountable, even if it is troublesome, and even if reworking existing inventory isn't deemed practical.

On balance, this analysis comes down to very attractive incremental short-run profits, coupled with some qualitative caveats which mitigate, somewhat, this attractiveness, and a major financing concern which may or may not be deemed binding. The case is sufficiently rich that managers very seldom go outside this relevant cost framework in considering the decision. The case reinforces many basic managerial accounting themes, such as

- Cost behavior analysis.
- Profit contribution analysis.
- Long-run versus short-run product and customer profitability.
- Inventory and receivables carrying cost.
- Working capital management.
- Project return on investment (ROA versus residual income).
- Balancing quantitative and qualitative issues in a decision.

Also, it treats these themes in a context which involves sufficient marketing complexity (the erosion issue, and the private label volume enhancement idea for makers of branded products), and sufficient uncertainty (the short-term debt crunch and the structure of the consigned inventory provision) that it will support excellent discussion with senior management groups. In fact, we have used the case more than 30 times in programs for eight major corporations and in the Dartmouth Senior Executive Seminar. The relevant cost framework is the one which emerges in virtually every discussion.

STRATEGIC ANALYSIS OF THE HI-VALU OFFER

We are not aware of many cases in which the strategic cost analysis yields such totally different insights from the managerial accounting analysis. Because the two perspectives diverge so widely here, this case is very useful for demonstrating how dangerously narrow our conventional viewpoint can sometimes be. It is interesting to note that virtually none of the points we will mention in this section of the paper are typically raised by the more than 1,000 senior level managers with whom we have used the case. This is not a criticism of these managers; rather, it is a comment on the prevailing narrow conception of cost analysis among American businesses.

A strategic analysis should start by looking at the likely positioning of the Challenger bike in the marketplace and the likely penetration it will achieve. This follows the fundamental logic of marketing strategy: segmentation and positioning. Although the case is silent on the segmentation issue and on the differing basic economics of a middle America retailer (Baldwin's normal customer) versus a discount chain (HV), it is not difficult to speculate on these subjects with reasonable accuracy. The fact that the case is totally silent on these issues is further evidence of what contemporary managerial accounting authors see as relevant concerns. Based on general knowledge of retailers' profit margins and some estimating of freight costs, it is possible to construct the following strategic cost comparison:

	One of Baldwin's Current Dealers		Hi-Valu Stores	
Purchase cost		$110		$ 92
Freight cost		10	(Truckload shipping)	8
Delivered cost		120		100
Necessary margin as percent of sales price	(Independent retailer)	40%	(Discount merchandiser)	25%
Implied retail price		$200		$133

Is this difference of $67 reflective of a commensurate difference in value to the consumer? It should be noted that the bikes themselves only differ in cosmetic ways. The basic elements which drive the value of the bike are identical (weight to strength relationship in the frame, derailleur, crankshaft, gears, and brakes). Other elements of "real" value (free assembly, point of sale merchandising, service) or "perceived" value (brand image, dealer image) do obviously differ between the two products. But, do they differ by $67 worth on a $200 purchase!? This is a *real* issue.

It is also possible to develop a simple market segmentation, based on general knowledge about bicycle retailing, as shown in Exhibit 1–1. This segmentation immediately raises the issue of whether HV's positioning of the Challenger bike will attract customers from the "cheap" bike segment

EXHIBIT 1–1   Market Segmentation

Retail Pricing, (1982)		*Suppliers*
($300 and up fast)	I. "Premium" bike High price/High quality ——————— Sold through bike stores	Fuji Bianci Univega Peugot Trek ⋮
($150–$250)	II. "Value" bike Midprice/Midquality ——————— Sold through hardware, toys, sporting goods stores, department stores ↓ ?	Schwinn Huffy Murray Ross Raleigh Columbia Baldwin ⋮
	[Low price/Midquality ——————— Hi-Valu, Sears, Penneys]	Private labels
($100±)	↑ ? III. "Cheap" bike Low price/Low quality ——————— Sold through discount chains (Bargain barns, Caldor, Korvettes, Warehouse 19, . . .)	Generic brands Closeouts Distress stock ⋮

or the "value" bike segment. This distinction is critical for Baldwin. Challenger sales taken from low-end dealers (customers who trade *up* in quality for the *same* price) are totally new sales for Baldwin, but Challenger sales taken from mid-range dealers (customers who trade *down* in price for *comparable* quality) constitute a direct attack on Baldwin's mainstream business and on its mainstream dealer network.

Drawing again upon general knowledge of trends in retailing over the past few decades, it is very likely that a big share of Challenger sales will come from people who otherwise would have shopped in a neighborhood toy store, hardware store, sporting goods store, or small department store. Thirty years ago, virtually all bicycles sold in the United States were "value bikes." Specialty bike shops pushing premium priced bikes did not even exist and discount chains pushing the cheap, low-end bikes were just emerging. Sears Roebuck & Co. and J. C. Penney Company, Inc. were already well-established, but they were not perceived as a catastrophic threat to "mom and pop" retailers.

Over the past 30 years the bicycle business has developed almost exactly as Porter's competitive strategy framework would predict (Porter 1980). One can compete successfully by being different, and commanding a premium price for that differentiation—such as BMW in automobiles. Or, one can compete by being cheaper, and offering "reasonable" quality for the low price—such as Toyota in automobiles. A manufacturer who is neither identifiably better nor demonstrably cheaper will wither away over time, such as AMC in automobiles. Porter refers to such firms as being "stuck in the middle" because they do not have a sustainable competitive advantage. Such firms may survive for a long time if the *business* is sufficiently attractive (automobiles, for example) using Porter's five forces analysis and if growth rates and investment rates do not force a quick shake out of the weaker players (as they have done in microcomputers, for example). But, the firms that lack a sustainable competitive edge will eventually wither. Their future is behind them!

This analysis suggests that what Baldwin is really doing by putting HV into business is not only creating yet another direct competitor to its regular customers, but also offering that competitor a much better price than it offers its regular customers. Baldwin can, of course, argue that the Challenger bike is different, but what do we suppose HV will tell its customers?! And, what will the customers believe? Baldwin is almost certainly acting to further erode the already declining market position of its regular customers. In all probability, this is not a short-run, tactical profit enhancement opportunity. It is very likely a strategic repositioning with major long-run implications.

Just because the HV offer is a strategic opportunity rather than a tactical one does not mean it is necessarily unattractive for Baldwin. In fact, this sort of strategic repositioning may be just what Baldwin needs.

Cost analysis can play a significant role in evaluating this strategic opportunity. Examining the overall profitability of Baldwin is one way to assess the attractiveness of its current strategic niche. Looking at return on equity (profit/equity) in terms of margins (profit/sales), asset intensity (sales/assets), and leverage (assets/equity) suggests that Baldwin is currently marginally profitable, at best (Exhibit 1–2).

Baldwin is earning only about half of the average of all manufacturing firms even though it is much more heavily levered. A good case could be made that Baldwin presents too much basic business operating risk to justify such a high level of financial risk (leverage). Either Baldwin's lenders are asleep at the switch or they have been forced into the current situation by supposedly short-term loans that became long term, de facto, when inventory was not converted into sales. This strategic assessment of risk and return relationships makes it much harder to argue that Baldwin is a reasonable candidate for further loans.

Another use of strategic cost analysis is to flesh out the likely results, over time, of Baldwin's move into the lower price segment of the market. The company's basic economic structure currently is as follows:

- Contribution margin per unit $44 (40% of sales).
- Fixed cost base (annually):
  Manufacturing ~$1.5M   } $3.9M.
  Selling and Administration ~2.4M
- Break-even point = 89K units ($3.9M/$44) which is about two thirds of one-shift capacity.
- Profit (before tax) at 99K units would be about $440K (10,000 × $44). This estimate is quite close to the $474K earned in 1981.
- Profit (before tax) at one shift capacity of 133K units = 44,000 × $44 = $1.9M. This is *excellent* ROE!
- Asset investment:
  - Inventory = 120 days (obviously more an advocate of "just in case" than "just in time").
  - Accounts receivable = 45 days = typical.
  - Property turnover = 10.8/3.6 = 3x = reasonable.
- Fixed cost percent of sales:
  Manufacturing = 1.5/10.8 = ~14 percent.
  Selling and administrative = 2.4/10.8 = ~22 percent.
- Gross margin = ~26 percent of sales (2.8/10.8) which is very low for a consumer durables manufacturer.
- Selling and administrative cost = ~22 percent of sales, which seems very high for a low-margin manufacturer.

EXHIBIT 1–2 Return on Equity

	Margins (P/S)	×	Asset Intensity (S/A)	×	Leverage (A/E)	=	Return
Baldwin–1981	$255K/$10.8M (2 + %)		$10.8M/$8.0M (1.35)		$8.0M/$3.0M (2.67)	=	$255K/$3.0 (8 + %)
Average of American manufacturing (early 1980s)	5%		1.5		2	=	15%
Baldwin with the HV deal in 1982, at best	~$400K/$12.8 (3%)		$12.8M/$8.6M (1.49)		$8.6M/$3.0M (2.87)	=	13%

- There is a clear suggestion that Baldwin is geared up for a much higher level of sales than it is now achieving and that reasonable profit levels hinge on much higher volume levels.

It is, in fact, true that bicycle sales in the United States reached a peak of 15 million units in 1973 and had declined to 10 million units in 1982. It is thus not surprising that Baldwin looks like a company that sorely needs a lot more volume than it is getting. Does this not suggest that the extra volume provided by HV would be just what the doctor ordered?

We believe not—because we believe that the HV project is very likely to alienate Baldwin's current dealers. It is not only unethical, in our view, but also unwise to try to be a significant supplier simultaneously in two price segments with a substantially identical product. It is true that some industries do seem to try this ploy. The liquor companies do seem to make it work ("The only difference between $5 vodka and $10 vodka is $5 and a Russian-looking label"). But it has been a poor strategy for many other firms. Fram oil filters (Bendix) lost their ability to command a premium price when they became so readily available in discount chains. Chevrolet and Oldsmobile were totally different automobiles in the 1950s. Many people believe that much of GM's current decline can be traced to the decision to stop differentiating its cars in ways other than cosmetic trim and price. GM even lost a court case over the use of Chevrolet engines in Oldsmobiles. The company saw this as just a normal part of its "common parts" manufacturing strategy. Consumers saw it as breaking faith with the Oldsmobile tradition. The Toro Company almost went bankrupt in 1980 when it "solved" an excess inventory problem by flooding discount chains with its supposedly premium snow blowers. It almost lost its dealer network in the process.

Baldwin's dealers cannot stop the firm from supplying HV, but they do not have to cooperate with HV's strategy by offering the $200 Baldwin bike as the "stalking horse" for the $133 Challenger bike. If they normally stock two or three brands, to give their customers a choice, they can add Huffy or Ross or Murray or Schwinn and drop Baldwin from the set. This would, in effect, drive Baldwin much more heavily toward the still growing low-end bike segment and away from the declining mid-value segment. What would this change in Baldwin's sales mix do for its basic economics?

- Contribution margin would only be $23 (25% of sales) instead of $44, and it would be likely to fall steadily via competition from the Taiwanese and the Koreans.
- The break-even point would now be 170K units ($3.9M/$23). This is about 130 percent of one shift capacity (break-even point greater than capacity is one pretty sure strategic danger signal!).

- If there are good reasons to stay with a one-shift operation and if the firm wants to earn 15 percent ROE, on a $3M equity base, it must earn $450K after tax or $900K before tax. This requires ~39K bicycles (at $23 contribution each).
- This leaves ~94K bikes to pay for fixed overhead (133K − 39K). At $23 per bike, this allows ~$2.2M for overhead (94K × $23).
- Thus, the firm will have to cut its fixed costs by more than 40 percent, in the *short* run (from $3.9M to $2.2M), just to earn an average return on equity!
- As prices come under continuing pressure from foreign manufacturers, unless Baldwin can cut variable costs, margins will fall and overhead will have to be cut even more.

Can Baldwin realistically expect to compete as a supplier of low cost bikes once the attraction of its mid-range brand image has been eroded away? What would be the possible source of its cost advantage? Very few American firms have learned to play this game well, especially when starting from a weakened position such as Baldwin faces. Thus, the cold reality is that Baldwin is caught between the proverbial rock and hard place! Its position can be summarized as follows:

- It is profitable, but only modestly so.
- It is heavily leveraged—probably too heavily.
- Its strategic niche is eroding away, slowly but surely.
- A "solution" presents itself (the HV offer).

Plus

- Looks like great Δ RI
- Utilizes excess capacity
- Opens new channel of distribution for Baldwin that is a "growth market"

Minus

- Looks extremely profitable for HV. Can we negotiate a *better* deal?
  [Probably yes, but should we try?]
- Raises major ethical issues about our responsibility to our current customers
- Barely breakeven on full cost basis
- Major cash flow crunch—can we borrow Δ $600K?
- At best, puts company ROE at "average" level
- *Strategically very risky*

**What looks like a good opportunity from a short-run relevant
cost perspective looks like a disaster from a strategic perspective.**

Exhibit 1–3 summarizes the strategic options from a financial perspective. How can cost analysis help the firm to understand the relative
attractiveness of the strategic alternatives?

Baldwin clearly cannot plan to stay in their current niche indefinitely
nor can they move 100 percent to the HV niche. What other strategic
alternatives do they have? How can cost analysis help the firm to assess
the relative attractiveness of these options? Additional strategic alternatives would be:

1. Go 100 percent to "Premium" segment.

2. Try to find new product opportunities in the value niche (mountain
   bikes, etc.)

EXHIBIT 1–3   Strategic Cost Analysis for Baldwin

Alternative #1   Do not accept the HV deal
  - ROE is inadequate (~ 8%)
  - "Middle market" is slowly shrinking (e.g., Gimbels caught between
    Bloomingdales and Marshals).
  - Even if we reject the HV offer, someone else will do it, thereby further
    eroding our current niche. So, even our current ROE of 8 percent is
    vulnerable.

Alternative #2   Current niche + HV Deal
  - ROE is still average (~ 13%) at best.
  - Great threat to the "core" business. If our dealers drop our product, the
    projected ROE of 13 percent is seriously open to question. We might be
    forced to go 100 percent HV, where the basic economics are marginal, at
    best, for us.
  - What if our current dealers ask for a deal similar to HV?
  - Going private label is a strategic shift; what are the organizational
    implications of diluting our strategic thrust?
  - Ethical issue: Is the difference in price of $133 versus $200 reflective of a
    difference in "value" to the customer?

Alternative #3   Go 100 percent to HV niche, or other discount merchan-
                      dising customers
  - Basic economics are marginal, unless able to cut fixed costs by more than
    40 percent, just in the short run.
  - Baldwin's ability to compete long run against foreign competition as a low
    cost producer is very doubtful.

There is not enough information in the case to do financial analysis of these, or possibly other, options.

Unless the firm can find a sustainable niche somewhere, its future is bleak. Some bicycle firms did find new prosperity in the middle 1980s in the emergence of the "off-road" bike which sold almost 3 million units in 1986. But the market research, product development, market development, and manufacturing retooling required to enter and succeed in this new niche probably would take far more money than Baldwin could muster. The firm has used up most of its slack chasing fond hopes of resurgence in a gradually dying market segment. Strategically, it is dead in the water, and it may not even know it! Other strategic options for the firm could be developed here, but that is not the intent of this analysis.

In summary, this strategic analysis, based heavily on concepts articulated in marketing strategy and in competitive strategy and using cost analysis designed to complement and reinforce the strategic view, presents a totally different perspective on the Baldwin Bicycle case. If we had access to the company's internal cost records and the records of its competitors and its customers, we could attempt a value-chain analysis to see exactly where Baldwin has gotten so far off the track. That is not possible in this case. What is possible, however, is to contrast even this rudimentary strategic cost analysis with the relevant cost analysis to show how different the business problem looks from these two perspectives.

We believe the cost analysis must be supplemented by strategic analysis in a case like Baldwin in order to understand the real business problem. This does not imply a condemnation of any of the basic tools of managerial accounting. Those basic ideas are as sound today as when they were first popularized in the 1950s. It does mean, however, that the cost analysis concepts must be explicitly tied to the strategic context of the business problem. In that sense, strategic cost analysis must now begin to go beyond managerial accounting just as managerial accounting went beyond the cost accounting framework it replaced 30 years ago.

DISCUSSION QUESTIONS

1. What major insights can you derive by focusing exclusively on the "relevant cost analysis" of the Hi-Valu proposal?
2. How do these insights differ when you explicitly adopt a strategic framework to analyze the Hi-Valu offer?
3. What strategic cost analysis ideas can you identify based on the Baldwin Bicycle Case? Are they generalizable? To what types of business decisions?

REFERENCES

Andrews, K. R. *The Concept of Corporate Strategy.* Homewood, Ill.: Dow Jones-Irwin, 1971.

Anthony, R. N. *Accounting*. Homewood, Ill.: Richard D. Irwin, 1956.

Buzzell, R. D.; G. Bradley; and R. G. M. Sultan, "Market Share—A Key to Profitability." *Harvard Business Review* 53, January–February 1975, pp. 97–106.

Hambrick, D. C. "Environment, Strategy, and Power within the Top Management Team." *Administrative Science Quarterly* 26, 1981, pp. 253–76.

Henderson, B. D. *Henderson on Corporate Strategy*. Cambridge, Mass.: Abt Books, 1979.

Horngren, C. T. *Cost Accounting: A Managerial Emphasis*. Englewood Cliffs, N.J.: Prentice-Hall, 1962.

Porter, M. E. *Competitive Strategy*. New York: The Free Press, 1980.

Snow, C. C., and L. G. Hrebiniak. "Strategy, Distinctive Competence, and Organizational Performance." *Administrative Science Quarterly* 20, 1975, pp. 546–58.

CHAPTER 2

Sheridan Carpets—Basic Cost Analysis Concepts Revisited Through a Strategic Lens

The major purpose of this chapter is to highlight the pitfalls of contribution analysis. Product-level marginal contribution information has gained widespread popularity in cost accounting textbooks as the basis for so-called short run decision making. It has come to be seen as *the correct way* to assess the profit impact of day-to-day pricing and product emphasis decisions. Since the fixed costs of operating the company do not change in the short run as the volume or product mix changes, the "correct" approach to maximizing profit is to maximize marginal contribution. This argument is absolutely correct at a conceptual level. At a practical level, however, given an intensely competitive market place, we have come to the conclusion that marginal contribution becomes little more than a convenient excuse to charge lower prices which all too often fail to generate an acceptable level of return on investment for the firm as a whole.

Examples of companies which have gotten rich using marginal cost pricing are extremely rare. On the other hand, examples of entire industries which have "competed" themselves to the brink of bankruptcy using marginal cost pricing are not hard to find (steel, airlines, trucking, paper . . .). For every strategically astute management decision which contribution information would facilitate, there are a hundred situations in which such information becomes the proverbial snare, trap, and delusion.

In one sense, it is certainly true that a strict focus on full-cost information represents a naive view of how costs really behave. In another sense, however, an emphasis on variable cost information represents an even more naive view of how managers behave based on reported costs. The history suggests that such information is misused and abused far more often than it is astutely used. Like an unfenced swimming pool, marginal contribution information is a "dangerously attractive hazard."

This chapter presents a case—Sheridan Carpets—where the incremental (or variable) cost analysis suggests a low-price, high-volume marketing approach. Use of the full cost metric and explicit consideration of strategic positioning points out the pitfalls of the penetration pricing approach and suggests the higher price as the more viable and attractive option.

SHERIDAN CARPET COMPANY CASE

Sheridan Carpet Company produced high-grade carpeting materials for use in automobiles and recreation vans. Sheridan's products were sold to finishers, who cut and bound the material so as to fit perfectly in the passenger compartment or cargo area (e.g., automobile trunk) of a specific model automobile or van. Some of these finishers were captive operations of major automobile assembly divisions, particularly those that assembled the top-of-the-line cars that included high-grade carpeting; other finishers concentrated on the replacement and van customizing markets.

Late in 1982, the marketing manager and chief accountant of Sheridan met to decide on the list price for carpet number 104. It was industry practice to announce prices just prior to the January–June and July–December seasons. Over the years, companies in the industry had adhered to their announced prices throughout a six-month season unless significant unexpected changes in costs occurred. Sales of carpet 104 were not affected by seasonal factors during the two six-month seasons.

Sheridan was the largest company in its segment of the automobile carpet industry; its 1981 sales had been over $40 million. Sheridan's salespersons were on a salary basis, and each one sold the entire product line. Most of Sheridan's competitors were smaller than Sheridan; accordingly, they usually awaited Sheridan's price announcement before setting their own selling prices.

Carpet 104 had an especially dense nap; as a result, making it required a special machine, and it was produced in a department whose equipment could not be used to produce Sheridan's other carpets. Effective January 1, 1982, Sheridan had raised its price on this carpet from $3.90 to $5.20 per square yard. This had been done in order to bring 104's margin up to that of the other carpets in the line. Although Sheridan was financially sound, it expected a large funds need in the next few years for equipment replacement and plant expansion. The 1982 price increase was one of several decisions made in order to provide funds for these plans.

SOURCE: Reprinted from *Accounting: Text and Cases*, Anthony and Reece, 7th ed., 1983, by permission of Prof. James S. Reece.

Sheridan's competitors, however, had held their 1982 prices at $3.90 on carpets competitive with 104. As shown in Exhibit 1, which includes estimates of industry volume on these carpets, Sheridan's price increase had apparently resulted in a loss of market share. The marketing manager, Mel Walters, estimated that the industry would sell about 630,000 square yards of these carpets in the first half of 1983. Walters was sure Sheridan could sell 150,000 yards if it dropped the price of 104 back to $3.90. But if Sheridan held its price at $5.20, Walters feared a further erosion in Sheridan's share. However, because some customers felt that 104 was superior to competitive products, Walters felt that Sheridan could sell at least 65,000 yards at the $5.20 price.

During their discussion, Walters and the chief accountant, Terry Rosen, identified two other aspects of the pricing decision. Rosen wondered whether competitors would announce a further price decrease if Sheridan dropped back to $3.90. Walters felt it was unlikely that competitors would price below $3.90, because none of them was more efficient than Sheridan, and there were rumors that several of them were in poor financial condition. Rosen's other concern was whether a decision relating to carpet 104 would have any impact on the sales of Sheridan's other carpets. Walters was convinced that since 104 was a specialized item, there was no interdependence between its sales and those of other carpets in the line.

Exhibit 2 contains cost estimates that Rosen has prepared for various volumes of 104. These estimates represented Rosen's best guesses as to costs during the first six months of 1983, based on past cost experience and anticipated inflation.

EXHIBIT 1   Carpet 104: Prices and Production, 1980–1982

Selling Season*	Production Volume (square yards)		Price (per square yard)	
	Industry Total	Sheridan Carpet	Most Competitors	Sheridan Carpet
1980–1	549,000	192,000	$5.20	$5.20
1980–2	517,500	181,000	5.20	5.20
1981–1	387,000	135,500	3.90	3.90
1981–2	427,500	149,500	3.90	3.90
1982–1	450,000	135,000	3.90	5.20
1982–2	562,500	112,500	3.90	5.20

*198x–1 means the first 6 months of 198x; 198x–2 means the second six months of 198x.

EXHIBIT 2 Estimated Cost of Carpet 104 at Various Production Volumes (first six months of 1983)

	Volume (square yards)						
	65,000	87,000	110,000	150,000	185,000	220,000
Raw materials	$0.520	$0.520	$0.520	$0.520	$0.520	$0.520
Materials spoilage	0.052	0.051	0.049	0.049	0.051	0.052
Direct labor	1.026	0.989	0.979	0.962	0.975	0.997
Department overhead:						
Direct*	0.142	0.136	0.131	0.130	0.130	0.130
Indirect†	1.200	0.891	0.709	0.520	0.422	0.355
General overhead‡	0.308	0.297	0.294	0.289	0.293	0.299
Factory cost	3.248	2.884	2.682	2.470	2.391	2.353
Selling and administrative§	2.111	1.875	1.743	1.606	1.554	1.529
Total cost	$5.359	$4.759	$4.425	$4.076	$3.945	$3.882

*Materials handlers, supplies, repairs, power, fringe benefits.
†Supervision, equipment depreciation, heat and light.
‡30 percent of direct labor.
§65 percent of factory cost.

INCREMENTAL COST ANALYSIS

Sheridan Carpets is a large player in the automobile carpet industry. It is a price leader, at least traditionally. The company faces a marketing decision for one of its high-grade carpet lines: Should they retain the price of product 104 at $5.20 or meet the competition at $3.90?

The incremental cost analysis would start by identifying the costs that would change if the volume is 65,000 square yards (at the $5.20 price) as opposed to 150,000 square yards (at the $3.90 price). Raw material costs are relevant (they stay at $.52 across all volumes in Exhibit 2). Materials spoilage, direct labor, and direct departmental overhead vary with the level of activity—as more of carpet 104 is produced, there will be more materials spoilage, more labor cost, more material handlers, more supplies, and so on. There are slight economies of scale in this business since variable cost per unit drops as the volume increases. It seems that the efficient plant size is around 150,000 square yards, beyond which there are diseconomies of scale.

Common sense would indicate that indirect departmental overhead (supervision, equipment depreciation, heat and light) are fixed costs. In any case, they are constant at $78,000 and do not vary with activity levels.

General overhead probably includes items like plant insurance, property taxes, plant depreciation, factory personnel department, etc. These costs are incurred for all of Sheridan's carpet lines, including 104. Further, product 104 represents only 3 percent of the total sales of the com-

TABLE 2–1   Contribution Analysis

	Selling Price per Unit			
	$3.90		$5.20	
Variable cost per unit:				
Raw materials	$.52		$ .52	
Materials spoilage	.05		.05	
Direct labor	.96		1.03	
Department direct overhead	.13	$1.66	.14	$1.74
Contribution per unit		$2.24		$3.46
Volume		150,000 sq. yds.		65,000 sq. yds.
Total contribution		$335,850		$224,900

Note: The profit contribution numbers shown above crucially depend on the accuracy of the sales volume estimates at the two different prices.

pany (total company sales, $40 million; product 104 sales, $1.3 million). It is highly unlikely that general overhead would change for a volume swing of 65,000 units to 150,000 units on a product which represents only 3 percent of total sales. Thus, general overhead costs are not relevant for the current pricing decision. These costs behave like a variable cost in Exhibit 2 since they are allocated to products on the basis of direct labor, which is a variable cost. One can debate whether direct labor is the appropriate basis to allocate overheads. But this is a moot point since fixed costs are considered to be irrelevant anyway. Using a similar logic, one can exclude selling and administrative overheads since they will not change whether we sell 65,000 units or 150,000 units of 104, especially since salesmen are salaried.

Table 2–1 contains the profit contribution calculations for the two

FIGURE 2–1   Logic for the Contribution Analysis

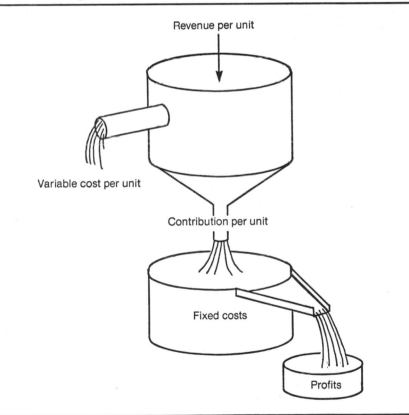

SOURCE: This figure was originally suggested by Professor Richard F. Vancil, Harvard Business School.

pricing options. Sheridan has greater total contribution at the $3.90 price ($335,850) than at the $5.20 price ($224,900). The logic behind the contribution analysis, i.e., the notion that maximizing total contribution is identical to maximizing total profits, is captured in Figure 2–1. When we say "contribution to fixed costs and profits," we imply that product contribution first flows into the fixed cost pot and only when that pot overflows, does it flow into the profit pot. Since the size of the "fixed cost pot" does not change between the two pricing options, the pricing option that maximizes total contribution is also likely to maximize total profits. Thus Sheridan should price 104 at the lower price, thereby maximizing both total contribution as well as total profits.

STRATEGIC COST ANALYSIS

The low-price, high-volume approach suggested above can be seriously challenged by a careful consideration of three issues: (1) Should the contribution metric or the full cost metric guide the pricing decision? (2) How should we incorporate competitive reactions to our pricing moves? and (3) How should cost analysis and strategic positioning be linked?

Contribution Analysis—The Braniff Fallacy

We will leave the analysis of Sheridan's situation for a moment and consider the arguments supporting contribution and full cost metrics. The contribution metric, however persuasive its logic may be, suffers from a major pitfall—what we will call the "Braniff Fallacy." Suppose the full airfare from Dallas to New York is $300 (full cost + return on investment). Let us further suppose that the plane is ready to leave Dallas and all but one seat is filled. Under this scenario, the incremental cost of that unsold seat is zero; all costs (such as pilot's salary, airplane depreciation, and fuel) are fixed. If that seat can be sold for $50, then there is a $50 contribution. The incremental view is probably justified in selling that seat at any "super-discount" price. However, selling just one seat adds, at best, $50 to the bottom line, not enough to make a big impact for a major airline. If the airline wants to make a big impact on its bottom line, it has to sell lots of seats with an incremental contribution of $50 per seat. However, if the airline follows this approach, it will have contribution, but *no* profit (since the fixed cost pot, as depicted in Figure 2–1, will not be filled up)! Here is the "catch 22." If the volume is large enough to make a big difference to the bottom line, then the incremental view is no longer valid— the so-called fixed costs (pilot's salary, airplane depreciation, etc.) have to be covered. One could argue that profitability in the airlines industry has been dismal during the past few years mostly because the airline companies are committing the Braniff Fallacy.

We summarize below the arguments supporting the contribution metric and the full cost metric.

Arguments Supporting the Contribution Metric.   Incorporating fixed costs on a per unit basis while making decisions is clearly suspect because:

- The resulting per unit amount is only accurate at one particular volume.
- It may confuse people by making a fixed cost appear to be a variable cost.
- It involves *arbitrary* allocation rules which cannot be justified or verified.
- It distorts cost-volume-profit relationships.
- Economic theory suggests that fixed costs are irrelevant for *short-run* decisions.

Arguments Supporting the Full Cost Metric.

- Economic theory suggests that fixed costs are relevant in the *long run* (all costs are variable in the long run). Full cost per unit (an "accounting" measure) is the best measure today of the long-run variable costs of a product.
- It is not clear when the short run ends and when the long run begins. Won't accumulation of short-run decisions result in a long-run impact? Will that not argue for a full cost view even for the so-called short-run decisions?
- In any case, many decisions have more long-run, than short-run, implications. There are very few purely short-run decisions.
- Fixed costs must be covered by the products in the aggregate, so *why not* charge each product for a "fair share."
- Whether a cost is fixed or variable is *within* a manager's control. If the incremental view is unduly emphasized, managers can convert all costs into fixed costs. For instance, managers can enter into long-term contracts to purchase raw materials and convert raw material into a fixed cost. Managers can adopt a "no layoffs" policy and convert direct labor into a fixed cost. And so on. It is a lot easier to sell a product focusing just on incremental costs, especially if the incremental product cost is zero!
- Looking at *incremental* business on an *incremental* cost basis will, at best, *incrementally* enhance overall performance. It cannot be done on a *big* enough scale to make a *big* impact. If the scale is that large, then an incremental look is not appropriate!

- Whereas "full cost" distorts the short-run perspective, "incremental cost" distorts the long-run view. Which is a bigger sin?
- Business history reveals as many sins by taking an incremental view as by taking a full cost view (remember the Braniff Fallacy).

Now returning to the Sheridan situation, the full cost per unit at all relevant volumes is greater than $3.90 (see Exhibit 2 of the case). Thus, under the full cost view, the $3.90 price will not even recover costs, let alone a reasonable return on investment. The $5.20 price appears to be the only profitable price. To recap, the contribution metric suggests the lower price whereas the full cost metric suggests the higher price. How can we decide between these two viewpoints? One possibility here is to view the problem from the competitors' standpoint.

Competitor Analysis

Table 2–2 presents a matrix where each axis measures the two pricing options for Sheridan and its competitors, respectively. If everyone in the industry prices at $3.90, Sheridan makes a total contribution of $335,800 (Box 1). If Sheridan stays at $5.20 and competitors stay at $3.90, Sheridan makes a total contribution of $224,900 (Box 2). If Sheridan lowers the price to $3.90, it is unlikely that competitors will increase the price to $5.20 (Box 3). If both Sheridan and competitors are at $5.20, Sheridan can potentially make $771,970 (or at least $530,850; Box 4). Thus, Sheridan is better off if competitors can be persuaded to move up to $5.20.

Where are the competitors better off? The relevant calculations are given in Table 2–3. If Sheridan prices at $5.20, competitors can either stay at $3.90 or meet Sheridan at $5.20. At the $3.90 price, competitors will make a total contribution of $1.2 million (even with a larger share of the total market). However, at the $5.20 price, competitors will make $1.7 million in profit contribution. Thus, competitors are better off at $5.20 as well.

If competitors are rational, they should increase the price to $5.20. Since Sheridan is the largest player in the industry, they probably have the lowest per unit cost. Since the $3.90 price does not cover Sheridan's full cost per unit, it is unlikely that price will cover the full cost per unit for the competitors. This would further strengthen the argument that competitors are unlikely to stay at $3.90 for long.

What if competitors do not meet Sheridan at $5.20? After all, competitors stayed at $3.90 when Sheridan increased the price in 1982. This could happen again. Under this scenario, Sheridan is better off at $3.90 than at $5.20 (Box 2 versus Box 1 in Table 2–2). But the full cost view does not justify the $3.90 price. What should Sheridan do? We need to consider Sheridan's strategy vis-à-vis product 104 in order to resolve this question.

TABLE 2-2   Contribution Matrix

	Sheridan	
	$3.90	$5.20
Competitor		
$3.90	① $335,800	② $224,900
$5.20	③ Not likely	④ $771,970* or $530,850†

Note: In the past, when Sheridan and the competitors were both at the same price, Sheridan had 35% of the market (Exhibit 1 of the case). Therefore the total contribution in Box 4 will depend on whether Sheridan can recapture its previous share of 35% of the market.

*35% market share			†24% market share		
Selling price		$5.20	Selling price		$5.20
Variable costs:			Variable costs:		
Raw materials	$ .52		Raw materials	$.52	
Spoilage	.05		Spoilage	.05	
Direct labor	1.00		Direct labor	.96	
Variable OH	.13	1.70	Variable OH	.13	1.66
Contribution per unit		$3.50	Contribution per unit		$3.54
Volume (35% of 630,000) = 220,500 sq. yds.			Volume (24% of 630,000) = 150,000 sq. yds.		
Total contribution		$771,970	Total contribution		$530,850

Strategic Analysis

Pricing is an important element of Sheridan's overall business strategy. Before making the pricing decision, we should therefore be clear as to what strategic objective Sheridan is pursuing vis-à-vis 104. Does Sheridan want to maximize short-run profits by pricing high ("milk the business") or does Sheridan want to increase market share, possibly trading off short-run profitability? Whatever the objective, it is critical that we

TABLE 2–3   Analysis from the Competitor's Point of View

Sheridan's price = $5.20

Competitors can price at	$3.90	*or*	$5.20
Industry volume	630,000		630,000
Less: Sheridan's share	65,000		150,000
Competitor's share	565,000		480,000
Competitor's variable cost per unit (assumed)*	$1.74		$1.74
Contribution per unit	$2.16		$3.46
Total contribution	$1.2 million		$1.7 million

*Since competitors are smaller than Sheridan, a variable cost estimate of $1.74 (Sheridan's variable cost at the 65,000 volume) for the competitors seems reasonable.

determine it explicitly. Otherwise the pricing decision would just be an aimless response to the moves of competitors. *What is Sheridan trying to do with 104?*

The Boston Consulting Group's grid (Henderson 1979) can be used to position product 104 during the early 1980s (Figure 2–2). Until 1981, the overall industry growth was modest (even declining) and Sheridan held the highest share of the market at 35 percent (Exhibit 1 of the case). This suggests that Sheridan was in Box 4 (Figure 2–2) in 1981, pursuing a harvest strategy with 104. Why then did Sheridan drop the price on 104 in 1981? It seems like a poor pricing decision for a harvest business, particularly since competitors are *very* likely to meet it.

Since 1981, the industry demand has been growing and Sheridan's share of this market is at 10 percent by 1983. Thus, product 104 is in Box 1 (Figure 2–2) by 1983. The product strategy in this case appears to be to build market share in a growth industry and push the product towards Box 2. What is the appropriate pricing approach now?

Though lowering price to build market share has some appeal, Sheridan should stay at $5.20 and attempt to build market share for the following reasons:

- There is a reasonable probability that if Sheridan held the ground, competitors will increase the price to $5.20. Sheridan can then gain

FIGURE 2–2   Boston Consulting Group's Growth/Share Matrix

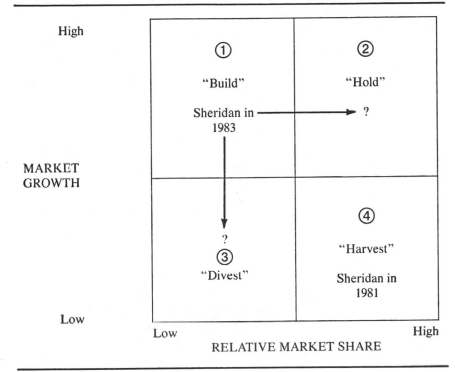

market share at attractive profit levels. Analysis of overall competitor sales volume suggests competitors may not have sufficient capacity to absorb 500,000 yards of 104. They are unlikely to build additional capacity to sell at $3.90.

- Product 104 is a high-grade carpet and should command the premium price, especially since (1) this product has no direct substitutes and (2) carpet represents a small percentage of the end users' cost structure.

- Since product 104 has a derived demand (depends on the demand for automobiles), it is unlikely that Sheridan can stimulate primary demand for 104 through price cuts. Any price cut by Sheridan will inevitably initiate a price war in which no one will gain.

- The full cost per unit does not justify lowering the price. At $3.90, there is contribution, but *no* profit.

- Pricing at $3.90 to gain market share and using that market power to increase prices in the future may be a very risky tactic since there is no assurance that the short-term losses can be made up in the long run.

Sheridan is therefore well advised to take the gamble at $5.20 and wait for competitors to move up to $5.20. When this happens, Sheridan will not only gain market share but would be able to realize a reasonable return on investment on product 104. This gamble may well fail, however. Sheridan is the one who initiated the price war; Sheridan first trained the customers to pay only $3.90 for good quality carpet; Sheridan trained some of its customers to use the competing product with no dire consequences in the end use markets; Sheridan created the market uncertainty which accompanies flip-flopping prices. Sheridan thus may well have ruined the 104 market for everyone!

If the competitors do not move up to $5.20, Sheridan needs to evaluate its strategy for 104. It is not necessary to build market share for every product in which Sheridan has a low market share in an attractive industry (for instance, General Electric divested its computer business in the early 1970s where it had a low market share in an attractive and fast-growing industry). If product 104 cannot be sold for $5.20 (to recover full cost + ROI), it should probably be divested (move from Box 1 to Box 3). The way to *real* success for Sheridan is to offer products that represent sufficient value to customers that they can command a selling price which covers not only incremental cost, but also a fair share of all the overhead and a fair return on investment (perhaps even an obscene profit once in awhile).

CONCLUSION

The incremental cost analysis for Sheridan advocated the low price approach. One of the objectives of this chapter was to challenge this conclusion by highlighting the complexities involved in choosing between the contribution metric and the full cost metric. At another level, the chapter emphasized the need to link cost concepts with strategy concepts, to derive the maximum value from cost analysis.

DISCUSSION QUESTIONS

1. Critically evaluate the arguments for and against contribution analysis in the context of resolving Sheridan's pricing decision?
2. What strategic cost analysis ideas can you identify based on the Sheridan Carpets Case? Are they generalizable? To what types of business decisions?
3. Think carefully about how you would reconcile marginal cost economic theory with full cost accounting theory. Are the two theories really in conflict?

REFERENCES

Andrews, K. R. *The Concept of Corporate Strategy*. Homewood, Ill.: Dow Jones-Irwin, 1971.

Govindarajan, V., and J. K. Shank. "Strategic Cost Analysis—Differentiating Cost Analysis and Control Depending on the Strategy Being Followed." *Journal of Cost Management*, 1988, pp. 2, 3, 25–32.

Henderson, B. D. *Corporate Strategy*. Cambridge, Mass.: Abt Books, 1979.

Horngren, C. T. and G. Foster. *Cost Accounting: A Managerial Emphasis*. Englewood-Cliffs, N.J.: Prentice-Hall, 1986.

Porter, M. E. *Competitive Strategy*. New York: The Free Press, 1980.

Shank, J. K. and V. Govindarajan. "Making Strategy Explicit in Cost Analysis: A Case Study." *Sloan Management Review* 29, Spring 1988, pp. 19–30.

———. "The Perils of Cost Allocation Based on Production Volumes." *Accounting Horizons*, 1988, pp. 2, 4, 71–79.

———. "Transaction-Based Costing for the Complex Product Line: A Field Study." *Journal of Cost Management*, 1988, pp. 2, 31–38.

PART TWO

New Concepts in Cost Analysis

CHAPTER 3

Concepts in Value Chain Analysis: The 'Famous' Crown Cork and Seal Company Case*

INTRODUCTION

Understanding and analyzing the "cost structure" of a firm is often the key to developing successful strategies. To quote *Fortune:* "Ask a second-year strategy consultant what he *actually* spends his time doing, and he'll tell you that 70 percent of it is devoted to studying the client's costs. How much, in harsh fact, does it cost to make a widget?"[1]

Both intuitively and theoretically, competitive advantage in the market place ultimately derives from "providing better customer value for equivalent cost" or "equivalent customer value for a lower cost." Thus, strategic cost analysis is essential to determine exactly where in the company's operations—from design to distribution—customer value can be enhanced or costs lowered. It follows that the accounting systems of a company must be designed to facilitate such strategic cost analysis—a function radically different from traditional record-keeping.

What is strategic cost analysis? Why is it important? How does it differ from traditional cost analysis? What modifications need to be made to the traditional cost accounting systems to facilitate strategic cost analysis? These issues will be explored in some detail in this chapter. The chapter uses the metal container industry setting, in general, and Crown Cork and Seal Company, in particular, as a way to motivate this discussion.

---

* A modified version of this chapter appeared in *Journal of Cost Management,* Winter 1989. Reprinted with permission.

[1]Walter Kiechel, "The Decline of the Experience Curve," *Fortune,* October 5, 1981, p. 140.

STRATEGIC COST ANALYSIS

What Is Strategic Cost Analysis?

Cost analysis is traditionally viewed as the process of assessing the financial impact of managerial decision alternatives. How is strategic cost analysis different? It is cost analysis in a broader context, where the *strategic* elements become more conscious, explicit, and formal. Here, cost data is used to develop superior strategies en route to gaining sustainable competitive advantage. Cost accounting systems form a critical part of the firm's infrastructure that allows the firm to select appropriate business, as well as functional, strategies. No doubt, cost accounting systems can help in other areas as well (inventory valuation, short-term operating decisions, etc.). However, the use of cost data in strategic planning has not received the attention it deserves, either in cost accounting textbooks or in management practice. There is a billion dollar a year market in strategic cost analysis consulting services dominated by such firms as Bain & Company, Boston Consulting Group, Booz Allen & Hamilton Inc., McKinsey & Company, and Monitor, Inc. Yet, not one business school in the country teaches a course built around the specific techniques used by these firms in this business niche. A sophisticated understanding of the firm's cost structure can go a long way in the search for sustainable competitive advantage. This is what we refer to as "strategic cost analysis."

Steps in Strategic Cost Analysis

According to Porter, strategic cost analysis involves the following major steps:

1. Define the firm's value chain and assign costs and assets to value activities.
2. Investigate the cost drivers regulating each value activity.
3. Examine possibilities to build sustainable competitive advantage either through controlling cost drivers or by reconfiguring the value chain.[2]

These steps are now considered in somewhat greater detail.

1. Identify the Value Chain.   Competitive advantage cannot be meaningfully examined at the level of the firm as a whole. The value chain disaggregates the firm into its distinct strategic activities. Therefore, the

---

[2]Michael E. Porter, *Competitive Advantage* (New York: Free Press, 1985).

starting point for cost analysis is to define a firm's value chain and assign costs and assets to value activities.[3] These activities are the building blocks by which a firm creates a product valuable to buyers. Activities should be isolated and separated if:

a. They represent a significant percentage of operating costs; or
b. The cost behavior of the activities (or the cost drivers) is different; or
c. They are performed by competitors in a different way (e.g., the on-board service at People Express versus American Airlines); or
d. They have a high potential of being able to create differentiation.

After identifying the value chain, a firm must assign operating costs and assets to value activities.

2. Diagnose Cost Drivers.   The next step is to identify the cost drivers that explain variations in costs in each value activity. The Boston Consulting Group (BCG) pioneered the concept of a "cost driver" with its notion of the "experience curve." According to BCG, cost per unit decreases predictably with the number of units produced (cumulative experience).[4] While BCG focused on a single cost driver, Porter[5] has argued that there are usually multiple cost drivers at work. Porter has offered the following set of 12 cost drivers: economies of scale, learning, pattern of capacity utilization, linkages within the value chain, linkages with suppliers, linkages with channels, interrelationships with other business units, level of vertical integration, timing, discretionary policies, location, and institutional factors. This list of cost drivers is not exhaustive but is representative of the factors that could explain variations in costs in a value activity.

3. Develop Sustainable Competitive Advantage.   Once the firm has identified its value chain and diagnosed the cost drivers of each value activity, the firm can gain sustainable competitive advantage either by controlling those drivers better than competitors or by reconfiguring the value chain (e.g., People Express and Southwest Airlines in the airline industry, Federal Express in air delivery, MCI and Sprint in long distance telephone).

---

[3]For diversified firms, the value chain analysis should be done at the business unit level.

[4]*Perspectives on Experience,* Boston Consulting Group, 1972.

[5]Porter, *Competitive Advantage,* pp. 70–83.

CROWN CORK AND SEAL COMPANY

We will illustrate the strategic cost analysis framework discussed above using the Crown Cork and Seal (CC&S) Company Case. Even though the case is about 10 years old, we chose to use it since our interest is to illustrate the strategic cost analysis ideas, not to provide insights into CC&S's current strategic position.

CROWN CORK AND SEAL COMPANY CASE

The Industry

With sales of $7.6 billion, metal containers made up almost a third of all packaging products used in the United States in 1976. Metal cans, made either from aluminum or tin-plated steel, represent the major segment within metal containers. Between 1967 and 1976 the number of metal cans shipped grew with GNP. The greatest gains were in the beverage segment (soft drink and beer cans), while shipments of motor oil, paint, and other general packaging cans actually declined.

Though there are about 100 firms in the metal container industry, it is dominated by four major manufacturers. Two giants, American Can and the Continental Can, together make up 35 percent of all domestic production. National Can and Crown Cork and Seal are also major forces with market shares of 8.7 percent and 8.3 percent respectively.

Because of the large number of competitors, the can industry is very price competitive. Since variable costs (material, 64 percent; labor, 15 percent; and freight, 8 percent) account for 87 percent of total cost, on average, there is very little operating leverage from extra sales volume. A new two-piece can plant costs only $10–$15 million per line and the minimum efficient plant size is two to three lines. There are few financial or "scale" barriers to entry.

Through the 1960s, American Steel companies were the sole suppliers of the metal used by the industry. Can companies, in turn, were the fourth largest consumer of steel. During the 1970s, aluminum came to dominate the traditional tin-plated steel markets. Also, of the four large aluminum producers, two have already forward integrated into manufacturing aluminum cans.

On the customer side, over 80 percent of output is purchased by the

---

Sources: Crown Cork and Seal Company and the Metal Container Industry, Harvard Business School, No. 6-373-077; Crown Cork and Seal Company, Inc., Harvard Business School, No. 9-378-024, 1977; and Teaching note for Crown Cork and Seal Company, Inc., Harvard Business School, No. 5-378-108, 1978.

major food and beverage companies. The can constitutes about 45 percent of total cost to beverage companies. Most customers maintain at least two sources of supply. Poor service or uncompetitive prices are punished by cuts in order size. Because can plants are often set up to supply a single customer, the loss of a large order from that customer greatly reduces efficiency and profits. Several food and beverage companies have already integrated backward into can production. Campbell Soup is a major producer of three-piece steel cans. The proportion of "captive" production increased from 18 to 26 percent between 1970 and 1976. This backward integration has taken place primarily in three-piece cans because buyers do not possess the technical skills to develop their own two-piece lines.

Early History of the Company

Recognizing Crown's position as the number 4 producer in an industry led by two giants, John Connelly sought to develop a niche strategy built around Crown's traditional strengths. He chose to return to the area he knew best—tin-plated steel beverage cans and aerosol cans, avoiding food cans and aluminum cans altogether. The supposed fate of a niche player in a commodity market is well known.

Crown had an early advantage in aerosols, since the company had developed the industry's first aerosol container in 1946. Little emphasis had been put on this line until Connelly spotted high-growth potential for the product in the mid-1960s.

In addition to the counterintuitive narrow product line, Connelly's strategy placed a heavy emphasis on solving customer problems. He actually wanted to "market" the commodity. In line with industry trends, he decentralized manufacturing, putting plants all across the country to reduce transportation costs and to be nearer the customers. Crown was different, however, in that it set up no plants to service a single customer. To better deal with rush orders and special requests, Crown purposely "overinvested" in additional lines, which were maintained in setup condition. In international markets Crown invested heavily in *undeveloped* nations which also violated industry trends.

Crown virtually eliminated all basic research, retaining only "applied" development focused on enhancing the existing product line. Crown was the only significant player not to spend significant amounts on R&D.

One of Connelly's first moves in 1957 was to pare down the organization. The company returned to simple functional organization. In 20 months Crown had cut the headquarters staff from 160 to 80 and eliminated 1,647 jobs or 24 percent of the payroll. As part of the company's reorganization, Connelly centralized all accounting and cost control while holding each plant manager fully responsible for plant profitability.

On the financing side, Connelly stopped paying dividends to conserve cash. He steadily reduced the debt-equity ratio, from 42 percent in 1956 to 18.2 percent in 1976, partly by repurchasing stock and partly by liquidating debt. He assiduously avoided growth for its own sake, remaining content to grow only as his market niches grew.

We were not able to break down CC&S's value chain because the analysis for CC&S relied solely on public sources which do not provide cost data by value activities. All the same, as we will see presently, the fact that important strategic insights could be derived based on an analysis of a somewhat aggregated value chain indicates the power of a full-blown value chain analysis. This section develops the following ideas in sequence:

Identification of Industry Characteristics

Here, we will concentrate solely on the structural characteristics of the metal container industry and leave any information about CC&S until later. We will organize the discussion using Porter's five forces framework (suppliers, buyers, substitutes, new entrants, and industry rivalry).[6] The net conclusion of this analysis is that the conditions facing metal-can manufacturers are extremely difficult and that the financial attractiveness of this industry is low.

Appropriate Overall Strategic Response

Given the industry structure and given that it is mostly an undifferentiated commodity game, one appropriate competitive strategy is to become *the* low cost producer in the industry. But, how can a firm cut costs in a commodity product? We argue that a strategic look at cost structure using a value chain framework can aid the firm to develop functional strategies to support the overall strategy of cost leadership. Crown Cork and Seal Company is such an example.

Identification and Analysis of Crown Cork and Seal's Strategies

Here, we demonstrate how CC&S has developed functional strategies by focusing on the major cost components; or in other words, how CC&S has done a *strategic cost analysis*. Clearly, the very impressive

---

[6]Michael E. Porter, *Competitive Strategy* (New York: Free Press, 1980).

financial performance of CC&S in a tough industry is no accident; rather, the success is attributable to the firm's ability to integrate cost analysis with strategic planning.

Structural Analysis of the Metal Container Industry[7]

According to Porter,[8] industry profitability is a function of the *collective strength* of *five* competitive forces: bargaining power of suppliers, bargaining power of buyers, the threat of substitutes, the entry of new competitors, and the rivalry among the existing competitors. To quote Porter: "The five forces determine industry profitability because they influence the prices, costs, and required investment of firms in an industry—the elements of return on investment. Buyer power influences the prices that firms can charge, for example, as does the threat of substitution. The power of buyers can also influence cost and investment, because powerful buyers demand costly service. The bargaining power of suppliers determines the cost of raw materials and other inputs. The intensity of rivalry influences prices as well as the costs of competing in areas such as plant, product development, advertising, and sales force. The threat of entry places a limit on prices, and shapes the investment required to deter entrants."[9]

The profit potential in the metal container industry is analyzed using the five-forces framework.

Bargaining Power of Suppliers
A. Aluminum Companies
  1. There are only four suppliers of aluminum (Alcoa, Alcan, Reynolds, and Kaiser); further, these companies are much more concentrated than the metal container industry.
  2. These firms have vast resources and pose credible threat of forward integration (in fact, Alcoa and Reynolds have already forward integrated into can manufacture).
  3. Can manufacturers do not pose any threat of backward integration.

Net Conclusion. Aluminum companies can exert considerable amounts of bargaining power over metal can manufacturers in negotiating raw material prices.
B. Steel Companies
  1. There are few suppliers of tin plated steel.

---

[7]Discussions on the metal container industry as well as Crown Cork and Seal Company are based on data as of 1977.

[8]Porter, *Competitive Strategy.*

[9]Porter, *Competitive Advantage,* p. 5.

2. Steel companies pose a credible threat of forward integration but have not actually done so yet.
3. Can companies do not pose any threat of backward integration.

Net Conclusion.   Steel companies can exert a good deal of bargaining power over metal can manufacturers.

Bargaining Power of Buyers (80 percent of metal containers are purchased by food and beverage companies)

1. Buyers of cans are very large and powerful.
2. The cost of the can is a significant fraction of the buyer's costs (the container constitutes about 45 percent of the total cost of beverage companies).
3. Customers buy in large quantities.
4. Customers buy an essentially undifferentiated product and face no switching costs.
5. Customers typically keep two sources of supply. Poor service and uncompetitive prices are punished by cuts in order size.
6. Can manufacturers typically locate a plant to serve a single customer so that the loss of a large order from that customer could greatly cut into profits.
7. There is low customer loyalty.
8. Buyers pose a credible threat of backward integration. In fact, several food and beverage companies already make their own cans (e.g., Campbell Soup is a major producer of three-piece steel cans). The proportion of "captive" production increased from 18 percent to 26 percent between 1970 and 1976. It is important to note that this backward integration has taken place primarily in the three-piece cans. The buyers do not possess the technical skills to develop their own two-piece lines.
9. Can manufacturers have no ability to forward integrate into the food and beverages industry.

Net Conclusion.   Buyers can exert a great deal of power over metal can producers.

Pressure from Substitute Products

A.   Aluminum

1. Its lighter weight could help in transportation costs.
2. Aluminum is easier to lithograph, producing a better reproduction at lower cost.
3. Aluminum is favored over steel as a recycling material, because the lighter aluminum can be transported to recycling sites more easily, and recycled aluminum is far more valuable.
4. Aluminum is known to reduce the problems of flavoring, a major concern of both the brewing and soft drink industries.

Net Conclusion.   Aluminum is a very great threat to the traditional, tin-plated steel (notwithstanding the fact that aluminum is about 20 percent more expensive than steel).

B. Plastics
   1. It is lighter.
   2. It is resistant to breakage.
   3. It has design versatility, thereby lowering shelf-space requirements.

Net Conclusion.   Plastics pose a significant threat to tin-plated steel in many user segments.

C. Fiber-Foil
   1. It is 20 percent lighter than steel cans.
   2. It is 15 percent cheaper than steel cans.

Net Conclusion:.   In certain user segments (particularly for motor oil and frozen juices), fiber-foil is a significant threat to tin plated steel.

Overall Conclusion.   With the exception of food cans, steel faces a significant threat from substitute materials such as aluminum, plastics, and fiber foil.

Threat of Entry
   1. Economies of scale in this industry are quite low and as such cannot be used as an entry barrier; for example, the minimum efficient plant size for two-piece can lines is two to three lines.
   2. Capital investments are certainly not an entry barrier (especially for suppliers and buyers); for example, for two-piece can lines the per-line cost is about $10–15 million.
   3. Technology is not an entry barrier for three-piece containers. However, the canning technology for the two-piece lines is not available with buyers such as Campbell Soup.
   4. Brand loyalty is absent and is not available as an entry barrier.

Net Conclusion.   Metal container industry has very low barriers to entry, as evident from the fact that this industry is characterized by a large number of small players.

Intensity of Rivalry among Existing Competitors
Notwithstanding the fact that there are only four major players in this industry (Continental Can, American Can, National Can, and CC&S), price rivalry is intense due to the following factors:
   1. This is a slow growth, mature industry (3 percent annual growth rate).
   2. Metal container is largely an undifferentiated product, forcing the customers to choose on the basis of price, if service is comparable.
   3. Presence of close substitutes keeps the lid on prices.

4. Low entry barrier puts a cap on selling prices.
5. Presence of very powerful buyers and very powerful suppliers keeps the container prices down (as otherwise they will enter the industry).

Net Conclusion.   Price competition is quite intense.

Overall Conclusion.   Given the very high supplier power and buyer power, low barriers to entry, availability of close substitutes, and intense price competition among existing players, the profit potential in the metal container industry is expected to be low. In fact, the *Forbes* magazine ranks this industry at 24 out of the total of 31 industries in the United States on the criterion of return on equity.[10]

Appropriate Overall Competitive Strategy

Given the commodity nature of the product, it is imperative that, to be successful, a firm in this industry must gain competitive advantage in relative costs. That is to say, a high performer must have *the lowest cost* in the industry. How can a firm cut costs in a commodity product? It can be done if cost analysis and strategic thinking are brought closer together.

The average cost structure in the metal container industry is estimated as follows:

Raw material	64%
Labor	15
Depreciation	2
Transportation	8
Research and development	2
General administration	9
Total cost	100%

The next section will discuss how CC&S was able to think strategically about the underlying forces that determine the magnitude of the above noted cost components and formulate functional strategies with a clear aim towards developing the least cost position in the industry.

---

[10]*Forbes,* January 13, 1986, pp. 256–58.

Identification and Analysis of Crown Cork and Seal's Strategies

We will first identify CC&S's functional strategies and then discuss their rationale by relating the cost structure of the industry to the strategic choices made by the firm.

Identification of CC&S's Strategies
1. Product/Market Scope:
   a. Overall approach: specialization.
   b. Focus on particular products: tin-plated steel cans (does not make aluminum cans).
   c. Supplying the needs of particular customer segments—beverages and aerosols (does not emphasize sales to food companies).
2. Manufacturing:
   a. Many smaller plants located near the customer.
   b. Have extra can forming lines (over and above dictated by economy of scale).
   c. Each plant serves more than just one customer.
3. Research and Development:
   a. No money spent on research.
   b. Follower, not leader.
4. Marketing:
   a. Quick turnaround on orders.
   b. Reward for new business.
   c. Sales representatives have single account responsibility.
   d. Equal treatment to all customers.
   e. Heavy emphasis on solving customer problems.
5. International:
   a. Aggressive penetration of international markets.
   b. Focus primarily on underdeveloped countries.
6. Organizational:
   a. Overall approach: "lean and mean."
   b. Centralized functional organization.
   c. Very low corporate overhead.
   d. Centralized accounting and control.
   e. Plant managers responsible for profits.
7. Finance:
   a. No dividends
   b. Low debt and buy back shares
   c. Reduce debt to equity ratio

CC&S's Choices: A Strategic Cost Analysis Framework

1. Raw Material Cost (64 Percent). Raw material is a very significant cost in the manufacture of metal containers. In the earlier discussion on the bargaining power of suppliers, we concluded that the suppliers (steel and aluminum companies) have greater bargaining power over metal can manufacturers in negotiating raw material prices. How was CC&S able to reduce its raw material costs relative to its other three major competitors? CC&S's strategic choice to concentrate on tin-plated steel helped the firm to reduce its raw material costs.

Though both aluminum and steel companies are more powerful than the metal can manufacturers, aluminum companies are *relatively more* powerful than the steel companies due to the following reasons:

  a. Aluminum companies are more concentrated than steel companies (4 aluminum companies versus more than 10 steel companies).
  b. Steel is more vulnerable to foreign competition.
  c. Metal container industry is the fourth largest consumer of steel products.
  d. Substitutes threaten the profitability of steel companies much more so than the profits of aluminum companies.

The above discussion implies that steel companies are more amenable to negotiating raw material prices as compared to aluminum companies. Therefore, CC&S's exclusive focus on tin-plated steel cans does give them a competitive advantage in raw material costs. Steel cans, also, are about 20 percent less expensive to make than aluminum cans. Further, CC&S chose to buy primarily from National Steel—a firm relatively more vulnerable among the set of steel companies. In fact, in the face of dramatically declining sales of tin-plated steel for cans (because of the inroads of aluminum), National Steel gave CC&S very advantageous prices in order to maintain sales volume.

Is there enough demand for tin-plated steel cans, given that aluminum offers significant advantages to beverage companies—the major customers for CC&S? It is unlikely that the beverage companies will completely switch to aluminum cans as long as aluminum is more expensive than steel. Further, a complete switch to aluminum cans would put the beverage companies more at the mercy of aluminum companies. Thus, there is likely to be "some" demand for steel cans. Continental, American, and National Can companies have exited the tin-plated steel can market, leaving CC&S the only player in this market. Thus, in fact, CC&S has been able to generate enough sales volume while, at the same time, keeping down raw material costs.

2. Labor Cost (15 Percent).   Labor is another major cost component for the metal container industry. CC&S has again found creative ways to reduce labor costs. In this industry, labor amounts to 15 percent of total cost while depreciation amounts only to 2 percent. This implies that substitution of capital for labor is likely to be very advantageous in this industry, since depreciation cost is much smaller in relation to labor cost. As it happens, a significant part of the time of the labor force is spent on "setup" because fast turnaround on rush orders is a critical success factor. In this industry, the customers—the bottlers—do not keep inventory of cans since the containers are bulky items to inventory and since the customers can dictate terms to the metal container manufacturers. It is not unusual for a semitrailer full of containers to be left at the fillers' loading dock for a day or two, and unloaded from the trailer and put directly onto the bottling line! Delivery is, therefore, extremely critical since failure to deliver exactly on time can foul up customers' highly automated bottling lines. In particular, a container plant that serves just one customer (as is true of CC&S's competitors) is very vulnerable to quick turnaround pressure.

CC&S's deliberate strategy to have extra can-forming lines is geared toward making an appreciable "dent" on the cost of "setup" labor since, with extra lines, laborers are not needed as often to change a line from one size container to another size container. No doubt, extra can forming lines add to depreciation costs; but these are more than offset by the reduction in setup labor costs. CC&S is the only player in the industry to have capitalized creatively on this labor/capital arbitrage opportunity.

In addition, CC&S's entry into underdeveloped countries is, in part, to exploit the cheaper labor costs in those countries.

3. Transportation Cost (8 Percent).   Because of the product's bulk and weight, transportation is a major factor in a can maker's cost structure. CC&S's manufacturing strategy of designing a plant to serve multiple customers increases its transportation costs as compared to its competitors who locate the plant close to a single customer to serve just that customer. However, as compared to its competitors, CC&S has been better able to neutralize buyer power through servicing more than one customer.

4. Depreciation (2 Percent).   Some of CC&S's strategic choices, as noted earlier, tend to increase the firm's depreciation costs relative to industry. However, two points need mention here: (1) the increase in depreciation cost is more than offset by reduction in other cost components and (2) the firm's strategy of reusing fully depreciated equipment in the international markets is likely to reduce its depreciation costs to some extent.

5. Research & Development (2 Percent).   CC&S's strategy of spending no money on basic research has enabled the firm to lower its R&D costs in relation to competition. But is it a smart strategy given the major technological changes taking place in the packaging industry?[11] It seems to make sense since CC&S is a much smaller firm as compared to Du Pont or Dow Chemical—firms which have a much greater stake in the packaging industry. CC&S simply does not possess the resources to invest heavily in basic research. Even if CC&S decided to spend 10 percent of its sales on R&D, it would still be "a drop in the ocean" compared to the R&D budgets of giants such as Du Pont. While CC&S's competitors spend about 2 percent on R&D, CC&S chose to use these resources elsewhere. History tells us that CC&S has been excellent as a follower. For instance, after two-piece cans were first developed by aluminum companies, CC&S was quick to adapt the same concept for making tin-plated steel cans.

6. General Administration (9 Percent).   CC&S has taken conscious decisions such as functional structure, centralized control, and very lean corporate staff to gain cost advantage in general overhead. As one example of this philosophy, compare annual reports for the major can companies. One is struck by the simplicity of CC&S's annual reports—no pictures, no fancy covers, just the financial details!

7. Overall Summary.   To sum up, CC&S's strategies have been carefully designed to reduce raw material costs (through choice of suppliers), labor costs (through manufacturing strategy), R&D costs (through R&D strategy), and general administration costs (through organizational strategy). These strategies, while giving the firm a competitive advantage in costs, have also helped CC&S to differentiate itself from the competitors along two dimensions: fast delivery (through extra can forming lines) and superior customer service (through the marketing strategy). Who wouldn't like to buy an inexpensive Mercedes?! This is an excellent example of how to build differentiation in a "commodity" industry.

In addition to the above noted areas of differentiation, CC&S's selection of target customers—beverages and aerosol markets—has given

---

[11]For a discussion of some of the more recent innovations in packaging, refer to "Want to Wake Up a Tired Old Product? Repackage It," *Business Week,* July 15, 1985, pp. 130–34.

the firm the ability to somewhat neutralize buyer power. The reasons for this are as follows: (1) CC&S is the largest supplier of filling equipment to the beverage industry and its expertise in packaging machinery gives it more credibility and access in selling cans to the beverages industry; (2) Aerosols build on the existing strengths of the firm since CC&S was the first to introduce the aerosol cans in the 1950s when CC&S was active in R&D; (3) The beverage industry is the fastest growing segment among the container users; (4) Though food companies use steel cans, CC&S did not emphasize this segment since advantages of backward integration were the greatest in the high volume, three-piece packer cans. But the threat of backward integration was the least in the two-piece cans.

The net result of CC&S's strategic thinking has been that the firm has consistently outperformed its much larger competitors, as illustrated by the following financial summary as of 1976:

	Continental Can	American Can	National Can	Crown Cork and Seal
Market share (1976)	19%	17%	9%	8%
Profit margin (1976)	6	5	5	9
Return on equity (5-year average; 1971–76)	10	7	12	16

Average return on equity of 16 percent during 1971–76 is clearly excellent!

The next section will discuss potential modifications that need to be made to existing cost accounting systems in order to facilitate strategic cost analysis as illustrated by the CC&S example.

TRADITIONAL COST ACCOUNTING SYSTEMS: NEED FOR REORIENTATION

Data generated from the traditional cost accounting systems are not appropriate for strategic cost analysis since they do not help the firm understand the behavior of costs from a strategic perspective. To quote Johnson and Kaplan: "Corporate management accounting systems are inadequate for today's environment. In this time of rapid technological change, vigorous global and domestic competition, and enormously expanding information processing capabilities, management accounting systems are not providing useful, timely performance evaluation activities of managers."[12] Several modifications, along the lines indicated below, need to be made to make the cost data a sound basis for developing strategies.

Identifying Cost Centers.   Management accounting systems accumulate costs by breaking the overall firm into several cost objectives or cost centers. Cost centers typically follow the organizational chart. To quote Horngren and Foster: "Costs are often routinely traced to a *cost center,* the smallest segment of activity or area of responsibility for which costs are accumulated. Typically, cost centers are departments, but in some instances a department may contain several cost centers."[13] It is possible to arrive at vastly different product costs for the same firm by varying the number of cost centers.[14] Yet, current writings in this area do not provide enough guidance in the setting up of cost centers except to say that they are the building blocks in cost accumulation. In fact, in a flexible manufacturing system (FMS) environment, the department ceases to be a meaningful concept.

The idea of a value activity—a concept almost identical to cost centers—is more precise from the standpoint of operationalization. Homogenous activities should be combined into a single value activity. Here, homogeneity refers to the fact that cost variation in that value activity is explained by a single cost driver. Thus, aggregation of activities with very different economics should be avoided. For example, it would be desirable to keep advertising and promotion as separate value activities since the relevant cost driver for advertising is market share whereas promotional costs are usually variable.

Value Chain Instead of Value Added.   Traditional cost analysis has focused on the notion of value added (selling price less cost of purchased raw materials) under the mistaken impression that this is the only area where a firm can influence costs. We argue that value chain—not value added—is the more meaningful way to explore competitive advantage. Value added could be quite misleading, at least for three reasons: (1) It arbitrarily distinguishes between raw materials and many other purchased inputs. Purchased services such as maintenance or professional consulting services are treated differently than raw materials purchased; (2)

[12]H. T. Johnson and R. S. Kaplan, *Relevance Lost: The Rise and Fall of Management Accounting* (Boston, Mass.: Harvard Business School Press, 1987), Preface.

[13]C. T. Horngren and G. Foster, *Cost Accounting: A Managerial Emphasis* (Englewood Cliffs, N.J.: Prentice-Hall, 1987), p. 87.

[14]Refer to Mayers Tap, Inc., 6-186-116, Harvard Business School, 1985, for an illustration of this phenomenon.

Value added does not point out the potential to exploit the linkages between a firm and its suppliers with a view to reduce costs or enhance differentiation (as we saw in CC&S); and (3) Competitive advantage cannot be fully explored without considering the interaction between purchased raw materials and other cost elements (e.g., purchasing higher quality, higher priced raw material could reduce scrap significantly and thus, lower total cost).

Comprehensive View on Cost Drivers.   Currently, direct labor hours is the most widely used basis on which overheads are allocated to products, under the assumption that direct labor hours is the most significant cost driver. This is an incorrect view. To quote Johnson and Kaplan: "For some cost centers, the number of direct labor hours worked will continue to be an important determinant of cost variation. But there could be many such cost drivers within a given cost center, or the cost drivers could differ across cost centers. For instance, machine hours may be relevant for highly automated departments, number of orders received or processed for the receiving department, number or some physical measure (pounds, gallons, square meters) of orders shipped for the shipping department, number of setups and pounds of material moved for an indirect labor department. Our goal should be to do the best we can in explaining the short-term variation in costs within each cost center."[15] Use of a single cost driver (such as direct labor hours)—instead of multiple cost drivers—can lead to erroneous strategic decisions, as illustrated below.

Decisions involving vertical integration strategies (i.e., make or buy decisions) could be incorrectly made if cost allocations based on direct labor hours are relied upon in making such decisions. To quote Eiler, Goletz, and Keegan: "For competitive reasons, many organizations are purchasing items that they previously manufactured. In such a case, once again, a direct-labor based overhead distribution technique becomes a company villain. The products that are *not* purchased absorb the costs of the purchasing department and of receiving, receiving inspection, and stocking. As a result, the cost system shows that it is better to buy than to make. Like a snowball gaining momentum as it rolls downhill, internally manufactured components become more costly."[16]

CC&S provides an example of a firm which has not relied upon a single cost driver but has used multiple cost drivers in achieving the low cost position: linkages (CC&S deliberately increased depreciation costs to induce a more than offsetting decrease in labor costs); policy decisions

[15]Johnson and Kaplan, *Relevance Lost,* p. 229.
[16]R. G. Eiler, W. K. Goletz, and D. P. Keegan, "Is Your Cost Accounting Up to Date?" *Harvard Business Review,* July–August 1982, p. 139.

(CC&S's policy decisions in the areas of R&D and organizational structure design enabled the firm to lower costs); and institutional factors (CC&S exploited factors such as tax holidays and financial incentives in the third world countries by penetrating those markets).

Excessive Focus on Manufacturing Costs.   Cost studies tend to focus on manufacturing costs. However, they are only part of the total costs of the product. Significant costs are incurred in areas other than manufacturing—particularly in sales, distribution, service, product development, and general administration. It is important to trace to individual products costs incurred in nonmanufacturing areas such as marketing and distribution. Evaluating product profitability based solely on manufacturing costs can yield inaccurate estimates of relative profitability. CC&S is an example of a firm which has realized significant payoffs by examining nonmanufacturing costs—in the areas of R&D and general administration.

Not Enough Attention on Fixed Costs.   Just as there is a tendency to be preoccupied with manufacturing costs, too much attention is given to variable costs and not enough attention is devoted to fixed costs. However, the so-called fixed costs have registered the most growth during the past two decades and, in some sense, seem to be the most variable! Also, truly volume dependent costs are less and less common in practice. Labor is no longer viewed as variable in many firms and virtually all costs are product and volume independent in a modern, automated factory. Thus, the distinction between fixed and variable costs appears to be less salient in today's manufacturing environment.

Also, material and labor have become a small part of the total cost to produce and deliver the product. For instance, direct labor at Hewlett-Packard Company is now such a small part of total cost (3 to 5 percent of sales) that they no longer keep track of it as a separate cost category. Labor is just a small part of overhead!

The above discussion leads to the conclusion that a careful scrutiny of the so-called fixed costs can yield major strategic cost advantages. CC&S provides an example of a firm which has benefited by thinking of innovative ways to reduce R&D and general administrative expenses—usually thought of as fixed costs.

Avoid Cross-Subsidy.   As noted earlier, it is critical that the costs in the entire value chain—from design to distribution—be traced to individual products. This obviously requires that common costs be allocated to products. Such allocations should be based on the relevant cost drivers and not based on simple allocation rules such as direct labor hours. Under simple allocation schemes, it is quite likely that some products will be overcosted and some others will be undercosted. This could seriously handicap the multiproduct firm since such cross-subsidies expose the firm to focused competitors who only compete in overcosted (and thus, over-priced) segments.

The problem of one product subsidizing the cost of another can be avoided if allocation of common costs is based on the relevant cost drivers—the transactions that actually cause the cost, whether it be direct labor hours, machine hours, number of setups, number of inspections, number of loads received, or number of parts change orders.[17]

Exploit Linkages.   Cost studies tend to analyze the cost of individual activities sequentially, without considering the linkages among activities that can affect total cost. Cost systems need to be designed in such a way that they highlight the linkages that exist among the cost elements across activities in the value chain (e.g., the system should recognize how spending on maintenance will lower machine costs). CC&S provides an example of a firm which has utilized the possible interaction between cost elements such as the linkage between depreciation and labor costs.

Avoid "Across-the-Board" Cost Reductions.   Typically, cost reduction efforts which are based on cuts of, say, 10 percent across the board are not likely to succeed for two reasons: (1) Such efforts do not recognize the possibility that deliberately increasing costs in one value activity can bring about a reduction in total costs (e.g., CC&S's deliberate decision to increase depreciation costs by having extra can forming lines resulted in a more than offsetting decrease in setup labor costs) and (2) Across-the-board cuts do not recognize the fact that different cost elements are influenced by different cost drivers. For instance, a firm's total volume might drop by 15 percent which could prompt it to cut support department costs by 15 percent. Such efforts are likely to fail if the product diversity has not changed since many of the support department costs are influenced more by product diversity than by total volume.

Reconfigure Value Chain.   While continuing the focus on controlling costs in the existing value chain, greater efforts need to be spent on redefining the value chain where payoffs could be significant. For instance, in the mature and tough meatpacking industry, Iowa Beef Processors has performed exceptionally well by controlling their processing, distribu-

---

[17]Such a sophisticated product cost system based on allocating different overhead items by different cost drivers was developed by William Boone when he was director of strategic planning at the Scovill Corporation. For a discussion of this system, refer to "Schrader Bellows," 9–186–272, Harvard Business School, 1986.

tion, and labor costs. They accomplished these cost reductions by *redefining* the traditional value chain in this industry. To quote Stuart: "Earnings per share (of Iowa Beef Processors) have soared at a compound annual rate of over 23 percent since 1973. The company has achieved this remarkable record by never wavering from its strategy and obsession—to be the low-cost producer of beef.

"To that end, it rewrote the rules for killing, chilling, and shipping beef. It built plants on a grand scale, automated them to a fare-thee-well, and now spends up to $20 million a year on renovation to keep them operating efficiently. The old-line packers shipped live animals to the abattoirs at such rail centers at Chicago, but Iowa Beef brought the plant to the cattle in the sprawling feedlots of the High Plains and Southwest. This saved on transportation and avoided the weight loss that commonly occurs when live animals are shipped. Iowa Beef also led the industry in cleaving and trimming carcasses into loins, ribs, and other cuts, and boxing the pieces at the plant, which further reduced transport charges by removing excess weight.

"The company has fought tenaciously to hold down labor costs. Though some of its plants are unionized, it refused to pay the wages called for in the United Food & Commercial Workers' expensive master agreement, which the elders of the industry have been tied to for 40 years. Iowa Beef's wages and benefits average half those of less hard-nosed competitors."[18]

Value Chain Analysis for Both Low Cost and Differentiation.   Strategic cost analysis is critical not only for the low-cost producer, but also for firms pursuing differentiation. To quote Porter: "Cost advantage is one of the two types of competitive advantage a firm may possess. Cost is also of vital importance to differentiation strategies because a differentiator must maintain cost proximity to competititors."[19] Needless to say, efforts at *simultaneously* reducing costs and enhancing differentiation would be the most desirable. CC&S was able to accomplish precisely this by reducing labor costs with extra can-forming lines while, at the same time, improving quality of delivery.

The above noted ideas in rethinking the development of cost information should not only be of interest to general managers and corporate planners who use cost data in strategic analysis but also to controllers who design cost systems as well as to cost accounting educators.

---

[18]A. Stuart, "Meatpackers in Stampede," *Fortune,* July 29, 1981, pp. 67–71.
[19]Porter, *Competitive Strategy,* p. 62.

DISCUSSION QUESTIONS

1. What major insights do you derive from the Crown Cork and Seal Case?
2. What is your understanding of the value chain analysis? How can such an analysis help improve strategic decisions?
3. Is the data generated from the traditional cost systems appropriate for value chain analysis? If not, why not?
4. What modifications are needed to be made to the traditional cost accounting systems to facilitate strategic value chain analysis?

CHAPTER 4

The Ajax Manufacturing Company—The Perils of Cost Allocation Based on Production Volumes*

INTRODUCTION

Business history is filled with examples of firms which have "bundled" their product offerings with explicit realization that profitability differed markedly across the bundle:

Gillette—razors and razor blades.

Kodak—cameras and film.

IBM—computers and maintenance service.

AT&T—telephones and telephone service.

In these cases, the less profitable (or even loss leader) segment was consciously used as a market entree. Individual product costing was not as important as overall bundled profitability.

Business history and current practice are also filled with examples of firms that make and sell an extensive product line while hoping to earn a profit on each item. These firms recognize the "value of variety" in attracting customers, but they also expect individual product prices to recover all costs and an adequate return on invested capital. In other words, these firms do not explicitly (or even implicitly) acquiesce in cross-subsidization of profit across the line. For example, General Motors recently announced a dramatic reduction in the complexity of its product offering (fewer models coupled with standard options packages). This reduction was apparently predicated on a fairly recent realization that the

---

* A modified version of this Chapter appeared in *Accounting Horizons*, September 1988. Reprinted with permission.

"cost of complexity" in their product line was not compensated by the value of variety.

For all of the companies which offer multiple products in a product line (or manufacture multiple product lines in common facilities) "accurate" product costing is critical to product pricing, product introduction, and product emphasis [Worthy 1987]. Explicitly managing the trade-off between the value of variety in the marketplace and the cost of complexity in the factory or the distribution channel requires an accurate assessment of product cost.

This chapter is intended to demonstrate how "traditional" and even "modern" approaches to product costing can be dramatically deceiving about product profitability. The "hero" is a concept called *transaction costing* which we will contrast with the "villain"—costing based on thruput or output volumes (volume-based costing, for short).

Transaction costing is certainly not a new idea. Recent references explaining it include Cooper (1986a, 1987a), Kaplan (1984), Johnson and Kaplan (1987) and Johnson (1987). But the concept is not widely used today because it is not widely understood or appreciated. Once the concept is widely understood, we believe transaction costing will replace volume-based costing as the approach taught in cost accounting courses and practiced in successful companies. Of course, that implies that the writings on cost allocation in virtually every existing cost accounting textbook are soon to become obsolete. This chapter presents a simple situation to illustrate the transaction costing methodology and, we believe, demonstrates its superiority. The chapter, of course, assumes that allocating indirect costs to products is a useful thing to do. That issue is not addressed here. An excellent reference in support of allocation, in general, is Zimmerman (1979).

AJAX MANUFACTURING COMPANY

The simplified case consists of unit cost calculations for three different products under each of three different cost accounting systems—"traditional" volume-based, "modern" volume-based, and transaction-based. The company and situation described here are highly simplified in order to keep the paper to a reasonable length. The situation is not hypothetical, however. For much more extensive examples of essentially this same problem see Cooper (1986b, 1986c, 1987b) or Shank and Govindarajan (1987). We will call the company Ajax Manufacturing, Inc. Ajax manufactures three different products for an industrial market. This constitutes a full line in the simplified context. The cost accounting system used by Ajax will be termed a *traditional* one in the sense that it is very much like the system literally thousands of firms have used for many years and still use today.

Sales prices and sales volume data for the three products are shown in Exhibit 4–1 along with basic production and standard cost statistics. Target sales prices reflect the prices needed to achieve the planned 35 percent gross margin, given the product costs generated by the accounting system (standard cost ÷ .65 = target price). The product costs are calculated as follows:

1. Charge each product for standard raw material cost (the sum of purchased components × standard price).

2. Charge each product for standard direct labor cost (standard labor hours per unit × standard charge per hour).

3. Assign overhead costs to units based on a *two stage* allocation formula. First (stage one), assign the costs of overhead departments to production departments based on some "relevant" measure of activity (square feet of floor space for janitorial cost, machine value for insurance cost, employee head count for personnel cost, etc.). Then, after all costs have been assigned to production departments, stage two is to assign costs to units of product based on some measure of "thruput" or output volume in the production departments. The most frequently used measure of production volume in multiproduct plants has traditionally been labor dollars (or labor hours).

In our example, since there is only one production department (machines), the first stage allocation is trivial. Since there is only one production department, allocating 100 percent of indirect overhead to it *must be* totally correct! Yet, even when the stage one allocations are perfectly accurate, meaningful product costing is not assured. The false belief that "reasonableness" of the allocations at stage one produces "reasonable" end-unit costs is part of the problem with volume-based costing.

Assuming setup labor is included, the total overhead to be assigned to the production in the machines department is:

Allocated overhead		
Set-up	$ 3,000	
Receiving	300,000	
Engineering	500,000	
Packing	200,000	$1,003,000
Directly assignable overhead		
Machines cost (10,000 hours × $70/hour)		700,000
Total overhead		$1,703,000

In a traditional costing system such as this, overhead is assigned to products based on direct labor dollars. Using this information, Ajax calculates the unit cost of products A, B, and C as follows:

Traditional Approach

		A	B	C
Raw material		$ 20.00	$30.00	$10.00
Direct labor		10.00	6.67	5.00
Overhead (labor $ basis)		75.70	50.49	37.85
Setup	3,000			
Machines	700,000			
Receiving	300,000			
Engineering	500,000			
Packing	200,000			
	$1,703,000*			
Total		$105.70	$87.16	$52.85

$$*\text{Overhead rate} = \frac{\$1,703,000}{\$225,000} = 757\%$$

Product profitability data can be summarized as follows:

	A	B	C
Standard cost	$105.70	$ 87.16	$ 52.85
Target selling price	$162.61	$134.09	$ 81.31
Planned gross margin	35%	35%	35%
Actual selling price	$162.61	$125.96	$105.70
Actual gross margin	35%	31%	50%

As shown here, Product A is achieving its planned margin. Product B is achieving only 31 percent gross margin because this product has come under heavy price pressure from foreign competitors. Ajax knows its factory is as modern and efficient as any in the world and thus is convinced that the foreign firms are "dumping" Product B in the U.S. mar-

EXHIBIT 4–1 Basic Product Information

	Product A	Product B	Product C	Total
Production	10,000 units in 1 run	15,000 units in 3 runs	5,000 units in 10 runs	
Shipments	10,000 units in 1 shipment	15,000 units in 5 shipments	5,000 units in 20 shipments	
Selling prices				
Target	$162.61	$134.09	$ 81.31	
Actual	$162.61	$125.96	$105.70	
Manufacturing cost				
Raw material	5 components @ $4 ea. = $20	6 components @ $5 ea. = $30	10 components @ $1 ea. = $10	

Labor usage*			
Setup labor	10 hrs. per production run	10 hrs. per production run	11 hrs. per production run	150 hrs.
Run labor	½ hr. per part	⅓ hr. per part	¼ hr. per part	11,250 hrs.
Machines usage†	¼ hr. per part	⅓ hr. per part	½ hr. per part	10,000 hrs.

Other overhead‡	
Receiving department	$300,000
Engineering department	500,000
Packing department	200,000

Note: There is only one production department, "machines," and it takes a little more than one labor hour for each machine hour (11,250/10,000) at the current product mix.
*Labor = $20/hr.; including fringe benefits.
†Machine cost = $70/hr.
‡Again, the categories of manufacturing overhead have been greatly simplified for purposes of this case.

ket. Ajax has dropped its price somewhat in response to the foreign firms, but it is very reluctant to cut further because of the low achieved gross margin. Its sales volume for Product B has fallen substantially, although B is still the highest volume product.

Fortunately for Ajax, it has been able to offset the declining profits from B by significantly raising the price of C. Ajax was pleasantly surprised when customers readily accepted the price increases here. Also, even with the higher prices competition has not challenged Ajax very much for this business. The result seems to be a very profitable low volume niche which competitors don't invade. Management presumes that Product C must have some unique characteristics which are very attractive for the customer, but which are not apparent to Ajax. Because of the market dominance it has achieved with C, Ajax should still be earning its target overall gross margin of 35 percent. But actual results seem to lag the projected results consistently. Management attributes the decline to inexplicable overhead "creep"—lack of discipline.

Concern with costs and prices for its volume leader, Product B, has led Ajax to experiment with some modern refinements to its cost accounting system. In fact a new approach to product costing has been developed by the controller, even though top management has not yet seen his calculations. Still using only the information in Exhibit 4–1, he has incorporated three refinements to the traditional system. His "modern" touches are:

1. Break out setup labor from the overhead pool and charge it to each product based on setup time per production run divided by the number of units in a production run. For example, for Product A, one setup costs $200 (10 hours × $20/hr.) and one run is 10,000 units. Setup cost is thus .02 per unit ($200/10,000). This refinement goes beyond averaging setup cost across the products to specifically identify it with the individual products. This refinement can be very important when products differ in setup time, or number of production setups, or in length of production runs (or all three).

2. Break out the overhead that is more related to material cost (receiving or inbound inspection, for example) and charge it to products based on material cost rather than labor cost. Under this refinement, there is a pool of material-handling overhead separate from the pool of production overhead. Material-handling overhead is charged to products based on raw material dollars, rather than direct labor dollars. This refinement can be very important when products differ in raw material content.

3. Substitute machine hours for labor dollars (or labor hours) as the measure of production volume. As factories have become much less labor-paced and much more machine-paced in recent years, the notion of

labor content as the best measure of "thruput" has lost its salience. When one worker tends several machines which perform different functions, run at different speeds, and differ markedly in cost and complexity, labor cost loses its meaning as a central element in product costing. The overhead rate of 757 percent (Overhead ÷ Direct Labor) for Ajax is a clear signal that labor is no longer a dominant cost component.

In fact, for this case, direct labor cost is only 8 percent of total cost, a far cry from the factory of our history or from textbook lore. When direct labor cost finally dropped to 3 percent of total cost in Hewlett-Packard, management relegated it to just another component of overhead in a two component cost system—material cost and overhead.

For Ajax, where the machines are ostensibly identical and machine-specific cost is three times as high as direct labor cost, machine hours consumed can well be viewed as a *better* measure of thruput and thus as a *superior* basis for assigning indirect overhead.

Using these three refinements, the controller has calculated product cost using standard raw material cost, standard direct labor cost, standard product-specific setup cost, material handling overhead charged in proportion to material cost, and production overhead charged in proportion to machine hours consumed. With these refinements, product costs of A, B, and C are as follows:

Modern Approach

	A	B	C
Raw material	$20.00	$30.00	$10.00
Material overhead (Material $ basis) (300K/700K = 43%)	8.60	12.90	4.30
Setup labor	.02	.04	.44
Direct labor	10.00	6.67	5.00
Other overhead (Machine hours basis)	35.00	46.67	70.00

Machines	$ 700,000
Engineering	500,000
Packing	200,000
	$1,400,000*

Total	$73.62	$96.28	$89.74

*Overhead rate = ($1,400,000/10,000) = $140/hr.

The controller is just about ready to present his modern cost accounting system ideas to top management. He feels sure that this information will further strengthen management's resolve not to cut prices on Product B any further. The new system shows that margins are even lower than management currently believes. The controller sees this as further evidence that foreign firms must be dumping Product B to Ajax customers. Part of his hesitation in releasing the new cost data had been based on his concern about how management would view the news that C is not really as profitable as they had thought even though A is much more profitable. This concern had lessened recently when he heard the sales manager say that Ajax was experimenting with even further 15 percent price jumps for C in some regions. Amazingly, salesmen had found customers still willing to order normal quantities. "C sure is a real winner," the controller thought to himself.

We will leave our narrative account of Ajax Manufacturing at this point to turn to a description of a much different system for allocating indirect costs—transaction-based overhead allocation. If only Ajax were aware of this system, they would see how painfully inaccurate their cost system is, even with the refinements the controller is about to propose. We will then consider how the transaction-based view of costs might lead to a dramatically different assessment of the options being considered.

Transaction Costing

In spite of the very good logic embodied in the controller's three refinements, the results still *fundamentally* misallocate overhead to products. Fundamentally, each component of overhead is caused by some activity. Each product should be charged for a share of the component based on the proportion of that activity which it causes. Production scheduling cost, for example, is generated by the number of production runs to be scheduled. It thus should be allocated based on the number of production runs each product generates. Products which generate a large number of relatively short production runs will *always* bear a less than proportionate share of the cost under any volume-based allocation scheme. Scheduling cost is not volume dependent in the short run. It is not even dependent on production volume in the long run. In the long run it is dependent on how many runs must be scheduled; not how many units we produce. Whether machine hours or labor hours is the better measure of output, *whichever* measure of output volume is used misstates the extent to which the product with many short runs causes scheduling cost. The basic idea is that transaction volume (number of production runs) is a better proxy for long-run variable cost than is output volume.

This concept is not particularly subtle or counter-intuitive. In fact, it is very much in line with our common sense. But, in earlier days, factories tended to produce fewer different products, cost was labor dominated (high labor cost relative to overhead), and products tended to differ less in the amount of support services they consumed. Thus, the transaction basis for overhead allocation was not likely to produce product cost results much different from a simple volume-driven basis tied to labor cost. Transaction costing would involve much more work and it was not worth the extra effort. Over time, the circumstances under which the more complicated transactions approach would produce comparable results have eroded. But eroding along with them was our awareness that volume-based costing is only useful when the simplifications upon which it is based are reasonable.

Helping to reestablish that awareness is the purpose of this chapter. There is no question that a transaction-based overhead allocation system adopts a long-run focus on cost behavior rather than short run. Transaction costing does not imply that overhead can be saved in the short run if the transactions which cause it are stopped. There is almost always a lag between changes in the volume of transactions and changes in the level of cost. Salaried production schedulers are not fired immediately if the number of production runs declines. Yet, over the longer run, scheduling cost is surely tied to one fundamental activity, one transaction—the number of production runs to schedule. A similar logic applies to each component of production overhead, such as shipping orders for shipping cost or receiving orders for receiving cost.

The transaction approach also disavows the notion that all overhead allocation is arbitrary anyway and thus is not worth trying to do "better." It presumes that meaningful allocation of fixed costs *is* possible and worth doing (Zimmerman 1979). In fact, the gradual rise to prominence over the past 30 years of the two concepts that full cost is less useful than variable cost and full costing is only an exercise in applied arbitrariness (Thomas 1969), also helps to explain why transaction-based allocation of fixed overhead has not received more serious attention.

In 1989, labor cost is not only dramatically less important, it is also viewed less and less as a cost to be varied when production volume varies. "Labor" is now part of the team in a large and growing number of companies. But business after business is choking on overhead. Indirect cost is now the dominant part of cost and businesses are desperately seeking ways to understand why its growth so undermines their efforts to generate adequate profits. In the prototypical "flexible factory," raw material is the only volume-dependent cost and the only cost directly relatable to individual products. A meaningful assessment of full cost in 1989 *must* involve assigning overhead in proportion to the transactions which generate it in the long run.

For Ajax, Exhibit 4–2 summarizes the distribution of cost-causing activities or transactions for each of the three indirect overhead departments:

Receiving orders for the receiving department.

Packing orders for the packing department.

Work orders for the engineering department.

This framework obviously simplifies a very complex phenomenon—determining what activities ultimately cause cost in any given department. Receiving cost, for example, is partly caused by bulk of receipts, partly by weight of receipts, and partly by fragility of receipts as well as by number of shipments received. For purposes of this example, however, the concept is demonstrated even though it is not fully amplified. The basic idea is that receiving cost is caused by receiving workload, rather than by production volume, and receiving workload for products may differ markedly from production volume.

Using this transaction volume to assign overhead to products is not difficult, once one has the data in Exhibit 4–2. Product A, for example, should absorb 4% of receiving cost ($12,000). Each unit of A thus should

EXHIBIT 4–2   Overhead Transactions Workload

	Product A	Product B	Product C
Receiving orders			
Receive each component once per run (a "just in time" inventory policy)	5 (4%)	18 (15%)	100 (81%)
Packing orders			
One packing order per shipment	1 (4%)	5 (19%)	20 (77%)
Engineering workload			
Distribution of workload in the engineering department is based on subjective assessment of long-run trends in number of engineering work orders for each product	25%	35%	40%
	[The standard, smooth running product]		[The complex, special problems product]

carry $1.20 of receiving cost ($12,000/10,000). In contrast, Product C should absorb 81 percent of receiving cost because it causes 81 percent of the receiving workload. Both of the volume-based systems *overallocate* receiving cost to products A and B because these products generate more production volume as compared to Product C. Unit cost now includes:

Standard raw material cost.

Standard direct labor cost.

Standard product-specific setup cost.

Machines overhead charge per machine hour consumed.

Indirect production overhead charged in proportion to the consumption of the transactions which, in the longer run, cause the overhead.

Following this transaction-based approach, unit costs for products A, B, and C are as shown below:

Transactions Approach

	A	B	C
Raw material	$20.00	$30.00	$ 10.00
Direct labor	10.00	6.67	5.00
Setup labor	.02	.04	.44
Machine overhead ($70/hr.)	17.50	23.33	35.00
Receiving (12K/45K/243K)	1.20	3.00	48.60
Engineering (125K/175K/200K)	12.50	11.67	40.00
Packing (8K/38K/154K)	.80	2.53	30.80
Total	$62.02	$77.24	$169.84

Managerial Implications

Exhibit 4–3 is a summary of product costs and product profitability for A, B, and C under each of the three approaches. The essential message is that Product C is dramatically undercosted under both volume-based systems while products A and B are overcosted. The two volume-based systems give a different rank ordering of cost for A and B, but both products are overcosted by both systems.

The general point is that the high-volume products will be overcosted relative to the low-volume products to the extent that overhead cost is

EXHIBIT 4–3   Comparison of Costing Systems

	Product A	*Product B*	*Product C*
Cost per unit			
Conventional volume-based system	$105.70	$ 87.16	$ 52.85
Modern volume-based system	73.62	96.28	89.74
Full transaction costing	62.02	77.24	169.84
Selling price	$162.61	$125.96	$ 121.55*
Profitability per unit			
Conventional system	$ 56.91	$ 38.80	$ 68.70
Gross margin	35%	31%	57%
Modern system	$ 88.99	$ 29.68	$ 31.81
Gross margin	55%	24%	26%
Transactions system	$100.59	$ 48.72	$ (48.29)
Gross margin	62%	39%	Negative!

*After the latest round of further price increases.

driven, in the long run, by transactions which are not proportional to output volume. In fact, much of the overhead in modern multiproduct factories is caused much more by the complexity of the product line and by the special handling of special low-volume items than by the volume of production per se. In these circumstances the high-volume products are either overpriced or show low *apparent* margins. Conversely, the low-volume products are either underpriced or show high *apparent* margins. The high-volume products are subsidizing the low-volume ones, but the accounting system camouflages the subsidy.

This opens the door for a niche strategy firm to attack the high-volume segment with aggressively low pricing. This firm will not have low-volume products to subsidize. It is thus possible that foreign firms are not dumping Product B at all. They just have a clearer knowledge of what B costs to make when it does not have to subsidize a low-volume special product like C. An all too common response by the full-line firm is to push even harder on the apparently profitable low-volume items. Their cost system indicates they cannot meet the competitor's low prices on the "standard" items and the special items always look very attractive at the margin. A convenient rationale for this action is the all too popular adage, "make something that really meets the customer's needs; don't just try to sell the things that are easy to make."

Like most popular aphorisms, this one has enough truth behind it to appear compelling. However, when it is coupled with an accounting system that systematically misallocates costs, it can spell disaster for a firm, like Ajax, that is not even aware it is acting unwisely. The more the low-volume special items are emphasized, the more the indirect costs will grow in the long run. But this growth is charged largely to the higher volume standard items which become progressively more and more unattractive, and the downward spiral of profitability continues.

The symptoms of a seriously flawed cost accounting system have been recently enumerated by Cooper (1987a). Many of them are present in Ajax:

> **Achieved gross margins are not easily explained.** Ajax cannot really explain its high margins on C very well or its low margins on B. The reality is that costs are misallocated between C and B.
>
> **Customers do not object strongly when prices are increased.** Given what it really costs to make C, customers have been getting a tremendous bargain. Thus, what Ajax sees as major price increases the customer sees as just a reduction in the amount of windfall. Product C is not so great or so unique, it is just dramatically underpriced!
>
> **What appear to be very high margin products are not attacked by our competitors. If the margins are so good, why don't we have more competition?** Transaction costing reveals why competitors are not rushing to offer C. Even with the projected round of additional price hikes, product C will still lose over $48 per unit! Ajax is much more likely to see competitors attack A than C.
>
> **Even though the product mix is moving away from apparently lower margin products toward apparently higher margin products, overall profitability is declining.** For Ajax the reported margins are an illusion. The reality is that the high-volume standard products have much higher margins than reported and the low-volume special products have much lower margins than reported.

Ajax cannot really mount an effective strategic response to its competitive problems because it is using seriously flawed product profitability information. A classic example of this phenomenon is documented in the recent series of cases about the Schrader Bellows Division of Scovill Manufacturing Company (Cooper 1986b). The dismal result for this firm was dismemberment following a hostile takeover made possible by poor stock market performance caused by declining profits. One Schrader Bellows factory produced 2,300 products which *all* showed up as profitable under their cost accounting system. Only 550 products were profitable once the transaction costing approach was applied. Virtually all the low-volume special items which looked very profitable under their modern volume-based costing system were, in fact, big losers under transaction costing.

Volume-based costing can seriously alter the way a firm looks at its strategic options and the way it assesses the profit impact of its pricing and product emphasis decisions. Transaction-based costing can at least clarify the cost dimension of such decisions. Armed with accurate cost information, the firm has a much better chance to construct and implement a viable strategy.

Until accounting educators and practitioners come to grips with the problems of volume-based costing systems and begin to provide realistic transaction-based cost data, we are aiding and abetting the charge that management accounting is part of the problem in American industry today rather than part of the solution (Kaplan 1984; Johnson 1987).

DISCUSSION QUESTIONS

1. What managerial insights result from the transaction costing perspective on product costs? Specifically consider:

   - Product pricing.
   - Product emphasis.
   - Most likely cause of the decline, over time, in control over overhead spending as the product mix shifted away from Product B and towards Product C.

2. Suppose a new competitor began to attack Ajax's position in Product A by cutting the price by 20 percent and offering customers very liberal payment terms. What would be the most likely response of Ajax management using their "traditional" costing system to measure product profitability? What would be the likely response of Ajax management if they were using a transactions-costing system to measure product profitability?

3. Suppose you are a consultant to Ajax Manufacturing. What actions would you recommend based on transaction-costing information? Be as specific as possible.

4. Can you anticipate resistance to adapt your proposed changes? From which managers? What action plans would you devise to overcome the resistance to change?

REFERENCES

Cooper, Robin. *Cases in Product Costing—An Overview.* #5-186-290, Harvard Business School, 1986.

————. *Schrader Bellows Cases,* #9-186-272, Harvard Business School, 1986a.

————. *Mueller Lemkuhl Case,* #9-187-048, Harvard Business School, 1986b.

————. "Does Your Company Need a New Cost System?" *Journal of Cost Management,* Spring 1987a.

————. *John Deere Company Cases,* forthcoming, Harvard Business School, 1987b.

Johnson, H. Thomas. "The Decline of Cost Management: A Reinterpretation of the 20th-Century Cost Accounting History." *Journal of Cost Management,* Spring 1987.

Johnson, H. Thomas, and Robert S. Kaplan. *Relevance Lost: The Rise and Fall of Management Accounting*. Boston, Mass.: Harvard Business School, 1987.

Kaplan, Robert S. "The Evolution of Management Accounting." *Accounting Review*, July 1984.

Shank, John, and Vijay Govindarajan. "Transaction-Based Costing for the Complex Product Line: A Field Study," working paper, Amos Tuck School of Business Administration, Dartmouth College, 1987.

Thomas, Arthur. *The Allocation Problem in Financial Accounting Theory*, Studies in Accounting Research #3, American Accounting Association, 1969.

Worthy, Ford S. "Accounting Bores You? Wake Up." *Fortune Magazine*, October 12, 1987.

Zimmerman, Jerald L. "The Costs and Benefits of Cost Allocation." *The Accounting Review*, July 1979.

CHAPTER 5

Transaction-Based Costing for the Complex Product Line: A Field Study*

INTRODUCTION

This chapter describes the application of "transaction-based" over-head allocation concepts in the Bellows Falls, Vermont mill of Monarch Paper Division of National Paper Company, one of the largest paper companies in the world. Monarch's existing mill-level cost accounting system is typical of those in the paper industry. Overhead is assigned to products through the familiar two-stage allocation procedure. In this industry, tons produced is the ultimate basis of assignment to products. As we will demonstrate, the Monarch system is subject to the same fundamental flaw which plagues any output volume-based allocation system when applied to a complex product line encompassing high-volume and low-volume products. Namely, the system averages away important cost differences among products by failing to charge particular products for the costs which result from transactions or activities which are caused by those particular products. When the high level of handling and processing activities associated with products that are processed in small batches are averaged across the entire product line, high-volume products are *overcosted* by a *small* amount (per unit) while low-volume products are *undercosted* by a *large* amount (per unit). The distortion is thus much more severe for the low-volume products. This distortion in product costs, in many cases, forces firms to choose inappropriate strategies. Low-volume specialty products appear to be significantly more profitable than they actually are, tempting firms to emphasize—incorrectly—the

* A modified verion of this chapter appeared in *Journal of Cost Management,* Summer 1988. Reproduced with permission.

low-volume business. This problem is widespread in American industry,[1] yet it is virtually ignored in cost accounting books. This field study is presented to further popularize the problem in the interest of generating a more widespread discussion of it among managerial accountants and accounting professors.

THE FIELD STUDY CASE

We run sales for this mill like a special order job shop, but we price most products like commodities, and then we use process costing so that everything gets averaged out!

Tom Beuthel, Mill Manager

In connection with its efforts to achieve a dramatic improvement in corporate profitability, senior management of Monarch Paper was trying in 1987 to develop focused marketing strategies for each of its 10 major paper mills. In order to achieve its target of 15 percent return on equity, the mills would have to double the 1986 profit figures without increasing investment—a very tall order! One location receiving particularly close attention was the Bellows Falls mill which produced coated and uncoated "specialty" printing papers (as opposed to high-volume commodity papers). Because of its specialty orientation, this mill seemed a good place to search for opportunities to achieve higher profit margins.

Within the mill, uncoated text and cover papers constituted the most complex segment of the product line. These papers were supplied to printers in many different finishes (linen, embossed, hopsack, vellum, etc.), different basis weights, different packages, and in a wide variety of colors. A particular basis weight and finish could be supplied in as many as 25 different colors, with each color available packaged in rolls, in sheets packed on skids, or in cartons. Considering basis weight, finish, color, and pack type, almost 400 individual selling items were offered to customers. It was accepted within Monarch that this variety was a necessary element of the marketing strategy. As one senior marketing manager observed, "We have to offer customers the entire spice rack. We'd lose much of our merchant business if we just tried to sell the salt and pepper." Being a full-line supplier was never really challenged very seriously.

---

[1] For some recent discussions of this problem see Cooper (1986, 1987), Johnson (1987), Johnson and Kaplan (1987), Kaplan (1984, 1986), or Shank and Govindarajan (1987).

Manufacturing managers often complained about the extra costs of making such a complex line of products, but the "value of variety" was widely assumed to offset the "cost of complexity." The extra costs of manufacturing specialty products were supposedly reflected in product costs under Monarch's cost accounting system and were apparently more than offset by higher selling prices. But the averaging effects which are present in any process costing system had never been closely examined. Mill overhead was averaged across all production on a simple per ton basis. It was thus not really clear that the low-volume specialty products were carrying their fair share of manufacturing costs. It was to this issue that a special "product complexity costing" study was directed in the spring of 1987. That special study is the subject of this report.

Uncoated text and cover papers were produced at this mill on three old, slow, small paper machines which comprised the "Number 2 mill." The plant also had three newer, faster, larger machines which, along with 22 coating drums, comprised the "Number 1 mill." All "sheet finishing" equipment (converting rolls of paper into sheets of paper sold in skids or cartons) was also located in the Number 1 mill. In 1986, production in the Number 1 mill was 119,000 tons of coated paper and in the Number 2 mill was 72,000 tons of uncoated white and colored paper. Exhibit 1 shows the range of reported product profitability for a few of the products produced on the #2 paper machine in the Number 2 mill. The extent of product proliferation for the Number 2 mill is summarized in Exhibit 2. As shown in this exhibit, despite the wide variety of products offered, 10 percent of the items account for 56 percent of the tons sold. The familiar "80/20 rule" is thus alive and well here.

All the production from the Number 2 mill goes first to the finishing section of the Number 1 mill and is then transferred immediately to the Distribution Center (DC) which is the stocking and distribution outlet for over 2,100 items produced at Bellows Falls and other Monarch mills. The DC employs 61 people and carries an average inventory of more than 18,000 tons of paper valued at more than $20 million. The DC is the largest paper warehouse in the world and is, in effect, a separate wholesale distribution business. But, for accounting purposes, it is treated as part of the Bellows Falls mill. All the operating costs of the DC are included as part of general overhead for the Bellows Falls mill. The DC is charged full manufacturing cost (but not carrying cost) for all the tonnage which it sells and it is credited for actual sales revenues generated. Its customers are wholesale distributors called *paper merchants* for whom DC becomes the primary inventory stock. Production from the Number 1 mill is shipped directly to printers and publishers without passing through the DC. In the product costing system, every ton produced at Bellows Falls is charged $21 for shipping and warehousing (see Exhibit 3), regardless of whether it is shipped directly to customers or passes through the DC.

EXHIBIT 1

MONARCH PAPER
Bellows Falls Mill
Grade Profitability Analysis, 1986*

| | | Cost per Ton | | | Profit per Ton | |
| | Annual | | | Revenue | Contri- | Fully Ab- |
Machine	Tons	Full	Variable	per Ton	bution	sorbed
⋮						
#2 paper machine						
⋮						
Monarch boxwrap grade 3 ream rolls						
White	32	$1,700	$1,074	$2,276	$1,202	$576
⋮						
Medium blue	41	2,335	1,642	2,953	1,311	618
⋮						
Canary	19	1,799	1,157	2,288	1,131	489
⋮						
Pink	45	1,830	1,138	2,343	1,205	513
⋮						
Russet	10	2,335	1,644	2,338	694	3
⋮						
Ruby red	40	2,346	1,645	2,995	1,350	649
Total grade (23 colors)	2,365	$2,053	$1,376	$2,442	$1,066	$388
⋮						
Total #2 machine	21,681	$1,168	$ 754	$1,344	$ 590	$176

*Excerpted from special mill grade profitability study done for business planning purposes in 1986.

Since $21 is a relatively minor charge, *on average*, this area is not deemed worthy of much careful analysis.

The product costing system at Monarch is typical for the paper industry. The standard cost for one particular product (Monarch Hopsack Cover—119 pound basis weight—lime color—packed in cartons) is shown

EXHIBIT 2

MONARCH PAPER
#2 Mill Production Complexity
1987 Plan

| | No. of Selling Items | Total Tons Sold | High Volume Selling Items | | | |
| | | | No. of Items | Percent of Items | Tons | Percent of Tons |
Machines						
#2	114	21,700	5	4.4%	12,900	59.0%
#3	149	23,700	18	12.1	12,200	51.0
#4	132	26,500	18	13.7	14,900	56.0
Totals	395	71,900	41	10.4%	40,000	56.0%

Note: 10% of the items account for 56% of the tonnage (the proverbial "80/20 Rule" is alive and well here!).

EXHIBIT 3

BELLOWS FALLS MILL
Current S&W Allocation Scheme
($ million)

Cost Center	1986 Budget
423–Traffic	$ 0.2
458–Motor trucks	0.4
493–Number 1 mill shipping	1.1
494–Outside warehousing	0.1
498–Distribution center	2.8
Services overhead	0.3
Total	$ 4.9 million
Total tons sold	231,000*
Shipping and warehousing per ton	$21.20 per ton

*119,000 tons from the Number 1 mill
  72,000 tons from the Number 2 mill, shipped through the DC
  40,000 tons from other mills, shipped through the DC
231,000 tons

in Exhibit 4. For the sake of brevity, we will call this product LLHC—shorthand for Light-weight Lime Hopsack in Cartons. As shown in Exhibit 4, the standard grade cost for LLHC consists of raw materials (pulp,

EXHIBIT 4

SAMPLE STANDARD COST PER FINISHED TON FOR ONE PRODUCT
(119 pound Hopsack Cover—lime color—packed in cartons)

		Standard Cost
Raw materials		
Furnish (3 different pulps)	2,229 pounds	$ 439
Additives (11 different items)	190 pounds	514
Tubsize	74 pounds	12
Broke credit	(296 pounds)	(15)
		$ 950
Paper machine		
#4 machine (.3215 hours/finished ton × $284/hour)		91
Paper machine overhead ($107.50/ton × 2,493 pounds)		134
Total rawstock		$ 1,175
Finishing cost		
Embossing		
Rewinding Σ (hours/finished ton × $/hour)		169
Cutting		
Trimpack		
Waste loss (493 pounds lost × [$1,175/ton − broke value])		235
Finishing overhead (Σ [$/ton × 2,493 pounds])		59
Carton packing		74
Shipping and warehousing		21
Mill level full cost		$ 1,733

---

starch, dyes, and additives), paper machine cost (LLHC is produced on the #4 paper machine), converting equipment cost (embossing, rewinding, cutting, trimming, and packing), a share of mill overhead, and the $21 per ton charge for shipping and warehousing. The quantity of each raw material item is derived from standard formulas to produce one ton of final product, allowing for waste and scrap. Component prices are from purchasing standards. Since scrap paper, which is called *broke*, can be reused to manufacture new paper, the value of the broke is explicitly credited to raw material cost.

Paper machine cost is calculated by multiplying standard machine hours per finished ton for this product (from detailed manufacturing reports) times standard cost per machine hour (labor and fringe benefits plus utilities costs plus maintenance costs).

Paper machine overhead cost is derived from a two-stage allocation process. First, all mill overhead is allocated to the production equipment based on detailed formulas derived by the cost accounting department.

Second, based on planned production levels for each piece of equipment, planned cost is divided by planned output to get standard mill overhead per ton. When this rate is multiplied by the number of pounds necessary to yield one good ton, the result is mill overhead cost per finished ton. There are actually three categories of mill overhead (production overhead, services overhead, and general overhead) in the Monarch costing system, but the three are lumped together here to simplify the example.

Converting cost per finished ton for the various categories of converting equipment used to produce LLHC is calculated in the same way as cost at the paper machine (standard hours per finished ton × standard machine cost per hour). The converting equipment overhead charge is calculated using the same two-stage allocation process as for paper machine overhead.

This costing system is viewed in the industry as being very sophisticated. The standards for each individual product for materials usage and processing rates (tons per hour) at each production stage are very carefully worked out. The allocation of mill overhead to each category of production equipment is also very carefully worked out. The idea that overhead should then be assigned to products on the basis of tons of thruput at each production stage has been generally accepted in the industry for at least 30 years. That such a system could dramatically misstate product costs is viewed as highly unlikely throughout the industry. Nevertheless, the system is seriously flawed for low-volume specialty products. The problem for these products is twofold: First, special handling and processing costs of the low-volume products are averaged across the entire product line, dramatically understating the true overhead cost per ton of the products which cause the transactions which generate this overhead. Second, the system ignores carrying cost. This is not viewed as a major issue in the industry since most production is shipped immediately against firm orders. The Bellows Falls mill is part of a group which shipped more than 1.4 million tons of paper in 1986. Less than 10 percent of that production is inventoried. In a context like this, inventory carry cost is just not a serious issue. However, for products which are regularly inventoried and are shipped from stock, carrying cost can be a major item.

The special "product line complexity costing" study for the Number 2 mill at Bellows Falls looked initially at only four categories of cost. The goal was to keep the study simple so the results could be easily interpreted. In essence, this is a not-too-complex first-cut at the distortions caused by product-line complexity. The four categories examined were:

1. Shipping and warehousing costs.
2. Inventory carrying costs.

3. Production control costs.

4. Production scheduling costs.

Each of these will be described briefly below.

Shipping and Warehousing Overhead Cost

The current allocation method for shipping and warehousing takes five specific departmental cost centers, plus the mill services overhead allocated to those departments and divides the dollar amount by the total tons sold out of the Bellows Falls mill. For 1986, this cost allocation yields a $21 per ton charge for each ton, regardless of whether it passes through the DC or is shipped direct (see Exhibit 3).

The new system for shipping and warehousing (S&W), as summarized in Exhibit 5, divides the overhead expense into three primary activities:

1. Shipping from the Number 1 mill.

2. Receiving at the distribution center.

3. Shipping from the distribution center.

As shown in Exhibit 5, the cost of the first activity, shipping from the Number 1 mill, includes all the cost centers (e.g., traffic, motor trucks, mill shipping, and outside warehousing) associated with shipping the paper to the distribution center or directly to the customer. Since *all* the paper produced at the mill passes through the Number 1 mill shipping department, the quantity shipped is the total production at the mill. Thus, every ton that passes through the mill gets charged an equal share of the $1.8 million of total Number 1 mill shipping cost ($1.8 million/191,000 tons = *$9.42/ton for shipping from the Number 1 mill*).

The cost of the second activity is driven by the receiving workload at the distribution center. Virtually all incoming shipments are packed on full pallets which weigh about one ton each (1 pallet = 1 ton = 14 cartons @ ~ 140 lbs. each). The DC employs 12 men in receiving at an annual cost of $453,000 (12 × $37,700). As shown in Exhibit 5, the receiving operation is also charged $364,000 for the other costs in S&W in proportion to the receiving workforce. Receiving thus carries a cost of $817,000 ($453,000 + $364,000). The Distribution Center received a total of 112,000 tons in 1986, so each ton received at the DC should be allocated $817,000/112,000 or $7.29 per ton.

The third activity is shipping the paper from the DC. Shipping at the DC involves two separate steps; the first is "picking" the order from inventory, and the second is loading the paper onto trucks for shipment.

EXHIBIT 5

COMPLEXITY COSTING STUDY
Shipping and Warehousing Study

		1986 Budget
1. Shipping from the Number 1 mill		
423–Traffic		$0.2 MM
458–Motor trucks		0.4 MM
493–Number 1 mill shipping		1.1 MM
494–Outside warehousing		0.1 MM
		$1.8 MM
Total tons shipped from the Number 1 mill =		191,000
Cost per ton	=	$1.8 MM/191,000
		$9.42 per ton
2. Receiving cost in DC		
Personnel cost		$ 453,000
Other cost		364,000
		$ 817,000
Total tons received at DC	=	120,000
Cost per ton	=	$ 817,000/112,000
		$7.29 per ton
3. Shipping cost at DC (picking and loading)		
Personnel cost		$1,094,000
Other cost		889,000
		$1,983,000
Total shipping items handled	=	177,600
Cost per shipping item	=	$1,983,000/177,600
		$11.17 per item

The DC employs 21 men for picking and 8 men to load the trucks. These 29 men cost $1,094,000 a year (29 × $37,700). As shown in Exhibit 5, other S&W overhead assigned in proportion to this workforce is $889,000 for shipping. Thus, the total cost of shipping is $1,983,000 ($1,094,000 + $889,000).

Since this activity is *not* based on tons, but rather on the number of items that must be picked and loaded, the proper allocation is dollars per *shipping item,* not dollars per ton. Each item ordered by a customer, whether it is 1 carton or 14, must be individually picked from the warehouse and individually stocked in the outgoing truck or railroad car. In 1986, the DC handled 177,600 shipping items. Thus, each item shipped from the DC should be allocated $1,983,000/177,600 or *$11.17 per item.* The cost per ton, then, is calculated by multiplying $11.17 times the average number of shipments required to equal one ton of paper.

By applying these costs to the LLHC product, we can calculate the complexity weighted cost per ton for shipping and warehousing as shown below:

1986 LLHC Data

Planned sales = 10 tons
Average cartons per shipment = 2 cartons
Average shipments per ton = 7 (14 cartons/ton ÷ 2 cartons/shipment)

Combining this volume data with the costs in Exhibit 5 we can calculate the S&W costs for the LLHC product in 1986:

		Cost per Ton
1. Shipping from the Number 1 mill (1 ton shipped to DC)	=	$ 9.42
2. Receiving at the DC (1 ton received at DC)	=	7.29
3. Shipping from the DC (shipped in 2 carton lots, 7 shipments = 1 ton. 7 × $11.17 = $78.19)	=	78.19
Total		$94.90/ton

Inventory Carrying Cost

The current costing system totally ignores the cost of carrying the inventory in the DC. For the LLHC product, 22 tons were stocked in the DC in 1986. This is more than a two-year supply! The heavy inventory results from running an "economic production quantity" in order to minimize production variances. This is a classic example of what happens when production cost is emphasized while carrying cost is ignored! The cost of money to National can be estimated as follows:

After tax (50% tax rate)
   Debt at 12% = 6% after tax × ⅓ weight = 2%
   Equity at 15% after tax × ⅔ weight   = <u>10%</u>
   Total   = 12% Before tax equivalent = <u>24%</u>

Using the current costing system for convenience, the 22 tons of LLHC represent an investment of $37,664, excluding S&W cost ($1,733/ ton − $21/ton = $1,712/ton × 22 tons). This represents an annual carrying charge of $9,040 ($37,664 × 24%). For each ton sold, this is a carrying cost of $904 ($9,040 ÷ 10 tons).

Production Control Costs

The Production Control (PC) department is part of mill overhead under the current product costing system. For the Bellows Falls Mill in 1986, PC cost was $1,090,000. Spread over the 191,000 tons produced, the *average* cost per ton was thus $5.71. But this average camouflages major differences across products in terms of the amount of production control activity a ton actually generates. In fact, of the 33 people working in the PC department in 1986, 13 were involved in work that varies directly with the number of *shipping items, not tons*. The other 20 people were involved in work that varies about equally between tons and shipping items. A further indication of the fact that overall tonnage is not as important as product complexity in determining PC workload is the observation that another mill of Monarch (with a much simpler product line) processes about 400,000 tons of paper a year with a PC staff of 6, whereas Bellows Falls has 33 people to process about 200,000 tons! Applying the PC cost at Bellows Falls in proportion to the transaction workload, rather than as an overall average per ton, yields the following breakdown:

1986 PC cost = $1,090,000
Headcount   = 33 people

Shipping items = 189,000(177,600 − #2 mill, 11,400 − #1 mill)
Tons produced = 191,000(119,000 − #1 mill, 72,000 − #2 mill)

Cost based on shipping items:
  13/33 × $1,090,000 = $429,000
  $429,000/189,000 = *$2.27 per shipping item*

Cost based on tonnage and shipping items:
  20/33 × $1,090,000 = $661,000
  $661,000/(189,000 + 191,000) = *$1.74 per weighted item*

For the LLHC product, the transaction-based PC cost would be as follows:

---

7 shipments per ton × $2.27   = $15.89
8 weighted units per ton × $1.74 = 13.92
  (7 shipments + 1 ton)
        Total cost/ton   = $29.81

It is worth noting that this cost is *more than five times* as high as the overall average cost per ton ($5.71) in the current cost system! The overall averaging system does not penalize the products shipped in small quantities for the extra work they generate in the PC department. The result of this distortion is that the high-volume products are overcosted by a small amount per ton while the low-volume products are undercosted by a large amount per ton. The distortion is much more severe on a per ton basis for the low-volume products.

Production Scheduling Costs

Production scheduling costs at Monarch are part of the overhead which is collected and reported at the group level rather than at the mill level. Production scheduling costs are thus excluded from individual product costs altogether since product cost includes mill level costs only. It is possible, however, to assign these costs to individual products because it is the products that generate the transactions workload which causes production scheduling cost.

The production planning department within production scheduling spent \$1,220,000 in 1986 (including direct costs and an allocated share of space costs, telephone charges, and computer costs). The workload in this department is based on the number of production runs to be scheduled. Because of the large number of production runs, the Number 2 mill at Bellows Falls generates a disproportionately large share of this workload. The department employs 28 people (for the entire Printing and Writing papers group) and 3 of them are assigned full-time to the Number 2 mill. Also, 1 of the 3 people assigned to the Number 1 mill works on the sheet finishing orders, for which about one half relate to the products of the Number 2 mill. For these 3.5 people, the workload is proportional to tons produced. Since Number 2 mill production was 72,000 tons, the cost per ton can be estimated at \$2.12 (3.5/28 × \$1,220,000/72,000).

In the sales service department, within production scheduling, cost is driven by the number of sales orders which must be processed. In 1986, sales service handled 224,000 sales line items shipped from the DC and 68,000 sales line items manufactured for direct shipment. Management in this department estimates that a manufacturing line item takes twice as much time to process as an item which will be shipped from stock. Total weighted workload units for 1986 can be estimated as 360,000 (224,000 stock items + 2 × 68,000 manufactured items). The 1986 budget for sales service was \$2,480,000 (including direct costs and an allocated share of space costs, telephone charges, and computer costs). The cost per weighted workload unit is thus \$6.89 (\$2,480,000/360,000).

Since the LLHC product is shipped from stock in two carton lots (on average), its sales service cost should be seven workload units per ton × \$6.89 per workload unit = \$48.23 per ton. Combining sales service and production planning gives a total production scheduling cost of \$50.35 per ton (\$48.23 + \$2.12). If one were looking at the Printing and Writing papers group as a whole, the average production scheduling cost per ton would be dramatically less. As noted earlier, this group produced and sold 1,400,000 tons in 1986. This would be an average production scheduling charge of \$2.64 per ton (\$1,220,000 + \$2,480,000 = \$3,700,000 ÷ 1,400,000 tons). The general point, again, is that items produced and shipped in small quantities are really dramatically more costly than average on a per ton basis because they involve many shipments to yield one ton of volume.

SUMMARY OF THE PRODUCT-LINE COMPLEXITY STUDY

Combining just the four categories examined in this special study, the LLHC product is *undercosted by more than \$1,050 per ton* in the current costing system! This difference can be recapped as follows:

	Current System	Transaction-Based Complexity Costing System
Shipping and warehousing	$21.20	$ 94.90
Inventory carrying charge	0	904.00
Production control	5.71	29.81
Production scheduling	0	50.35
Total	$26.91	$1,079.06

Difference = $1,052.15

In 1986, the LLHC product was selling for $1,526 per ton. With a reported cost of $1,733 per ton, it showed a loss of $207 on a full cost basis. However, since a large portion of the costs are not volume dependent in the short run, it was believed that LHCC showed substantial positive profit contribution. In fact, under National's costing system which considers only raw material cost and finishing labor to be volume dependent (~$1,300/ton for LLHC), the product showed ~$226 per ton of positive contribution in 1986. The business plan for 1987 showed a projected price increase of ~$21/ton and a projected cost saving of ~$112 per ton (~$23/ton of variable cost). This would leave the product with a full cost loss of only $74 per ton ($1,547 − $1,621) and a positive profit contribution of ~$270 per ton ($1,547 − $1,277).

As shown in the special study, this is a dramatically distorted view of the products' cost and profit position. Even granting the planned cost reduction and sales price increase for 1987, the product loses $1,126 per ton ($1,547 − ($1,621 + $1,052)) on a full cost basis. It even loses $634 per ton ($1,547 − ($1,277 + $904)) on a contribution basis!

TRANSACTIONS-COSTING: IMPLICATIONS FOR CORPORATE STRATEGY

What actions, if any, management will take as a result of this special study is still an open question. The positive impact on sales volume of offering a full line is still presumed to be considerable. But, the profit impact of that volume must now be seen in a much different light. It thus is no longer possible to argue that the value of variety *clearly* offsets the cost of complexity. The trade-off is often severe.

The situation described in this chapter is not atypical. It is widespread among U.S. firms. As just one major example, General Motors recently announced a dramatic reduction in the complexity of its product offering (fewer models coupled with standard options packages). This reduction was apparently predicated on a fairly recent realization that the cost of complexity was not compensated by the value of variety.

For companies which offer multiple products in a product line (or manufacture multiple product lines in common facilities), "accurate" product costing is critical to product pricing, product introduction, and product emphasis. Explicitly managing the trade-off between the value of variety in the marketplace and the cost of complexity in the factory requires an accurate assessment of product cost. In earlier days, use of volume-based measures (e.g., labor hours, machine hours, material dollars) to allocate overhead to individual products would have yielded reasonably accurate product costs for two reasons. First, a single factory typically produced a smaller range of products and those products tended to differ less in the amount of support services they consumed. Second, the percentage of nonvolume related costs (such as inspection, setup, and scheduling) was smaller. Thus, the transaction basis for overhead allocation was not likely to generate product cost results much different from simple volume-related allocation bases. Transaction costing was not worth the extra effort. Over time, the circumstances under which the more complicated transactions approach would produce comparable results have eroded. But eroding along with them was the general awareness that volume-based costing is only useful when the simplifications upon which it is based are reasonable.

The general point is that the high-volume products will be overcosted relative to low-volume products to the extent that overhead cost is driven by transactions which are not proportional to output volume. In fact, much of the overhead in modern multiproduct factories is caused much more by the complexity of the product line and by the special handling of special low-volume products than by the volume of production per se. In these circumstances, the high-volume products are slightly overcosted and the low-volume products are significantly undercosted.

This opens the door for a niche strategy firm to attack the high-volume segment with aggressively low pricing. This firm will not have low-volume products to subsidize. An all too common response by the full-line firm is to push even harder on the apparently profitable low-volume items. Their volume-based cost system indicates they cannot meet the competitor's low prices on the standard items and the special items always look very attractive. The more the low-volume special items are emphasized, the more the indirect costs grow. But the extra cost is charged largely to the higher volume standard items which become progressively more and more unattractive, and the downward spiral of profitability continues. Thus, the firm could potentially make a fundamental shift in its strategy from being a "full-line" producer to a strategy focused on "specialty" business, based on incorrect product costs!

The modern factory is characterized by dramatic product diversity and significant growth of nonvolume-related costs. We argue that allocation of costs related to complexity rather than output requires the selection of allocation bases that are also based on complexity measures. Better cost information can be provided by accurately identifying overhead cost with the products that generate the transactions which cause the overhead. Better cost information is certainly not a sufficient condition to produce better product decisions, but it is at least a necessary condition.

Management accountants and accounting professors must begin to consider problems like this one and proposed solutions to it, such as transaction-based costing, on a much wider scale in order to stay on the cutting edge of best management practices.

DISCUSSION QUESTIONS

1. The case describes the transaction-costing study conducted at the Bellows Falls, Vermont, Mill of Monarch Paper. What special problems and issues are you likely to encounter in collecting the raw data on cost drivers?
2. How would you summarize the major finding of the transaction-costing study done at Bellows Falls?
3. What implications does the new cost analysis have for the management of this plant? What specific actions would you propose based on this new information?
4. Draw up an implementation plan:
   a. Can you anticipate resistance to adopt your proposed changes? From which managers?
   b. How do you go about securing the commitment of those managers to your proposed changes?
   c. What time-frame would you adopt for implementing changes (two weeks–two months–six months–two years)?
5. What strategic cost analysis ideas can you identify based on the Bellows Falls case? Are they generalizable? To what types of business situations?

REFERENCES

Cooper, Robin. "Does Your Company Need a New Cost System?" *Journal of Cost Management,* Spring 1987.

————. *Cases in Product Costing—An Overview.* File Number 5-186-290, Boston, Mass.: Harvard Business School, 1986.

Johnson, H. Thomas. "The Decline of Cost Management. A Reinterpretation of the 20th Century Cost Accounting History." *Journal of Cost Management,* Spring 1987.

Johnson, H. Thomas, and Robert S. Kaplan. *Relevance Lost. The Rise and Fall of Management Accounting.* Boston, Mass.: Harvard Business School, 1987.

Kaplan, Robert S. "The Evolution of Management Accounting." *Accounting Review,* July 1984.

_____. "Accounting Lag: The Obsolescence of Cost Accounting Systems." *California Management Review,* Winter 1986.

Shank, John K., and Vijay Govindarajan. "'Unbundling' the Full Product Line: The Perils of Volume-based Costing." Tuck School Working Paper, Dartmouth College, 1987.

PART THREE

Differentiated Controls for Differentiated Strategies

CHAPTER 6

Kinkead Equipment Company, Ltd.—Profit Variance Analysis with a Strategic Focus

Profit variance analysis is the process of summarizing what happened to profits during the period to highlight the salient managerial issues. Variance analysis is the formal step leading to determining what corrective actions are called for by management. Thus, it is a key link in the management control process. We believe this element is underutilized in many companies because of the lack of a meaningful analytical framework. It is handled by the accountants in a way that is too technical. This chapter proposes a different profit variance framework as a "new idea" in management control.

Historically, variance analysis involved a simple methodology where actual results were compared with the budget, line by line (Phase I thinking). A major step forward was provided by Shank and Churchill (1977) who proposed a management-oriented approach to variance analysis. Their approach was based on the dual ideas of profit impact as a unifying theme and a multilevel analysis in which complexity was added gradually, one level at a time (Phase II thinking). Though Shank and Churchill's approach represents the best documented framework in the literature so far, we believe that their approach needs to be modified in important ways to take explicit account of strategic issues. Our framework (Phase III thinking) argues that variance analysis becomes most meaningful when it is tied explicitly to strategic analysis.

This chapter presents a short disguised case—Kinkead Equipment, Ltd.—to illustrate the three phases or generations of thinking about profit variance analysis. We believe it also demonstrates the superiority of Phase III thinking. The purpose of the chapter is to emphasize how variance analysis can be, and should be, redirected to consider the strategic issues that have, during the past 15 years, become so widely accepted as a conceptual framework for decision making.[1]

THE KINKEAD EQUIPMENT COMPANY, LTD., CASE

Andrew MacGregor, managing director of Kinkead Equipment, Ltd., glanced at the summary profit and loss statement for 1978 which he was holding (Exhibit 1), then tossed it to Douglas McCosh and looked out the window of his office overlooking the industrial center of Glasgow.

As you can see, Douglas, we beat our turnover goal for the year, improved our trading margin a bit, and earned more profit than we had planned. Although our selling costs did seem to grow faster than our turnover, all things considered, I would say 1978 was a good year for the firm.

Douglas McCosh, a recent graduate of a well-known European business school, was serving a training period as executive assistant to Mr. MacGregor. He looked over the figures and nodded his agreement.

Douglas, I'd like you to prepare a short report for the managing committee meeting next week summarizing the key factors which account for the favorable overall profit variance of 24,000 pounds. That might not be much for a firm like ours, but it would still pay your salary for quite a while, wouldn't it," he laughed. "I think you're about ready to make a presentation to the committee if you can pull together a good report.

Check with the financial director's staff for any additional data you may need or want. Just remember to keep it on a commonsense level—no high-powered financial double-talk. How about giving me a draft to look at in a day or so?

Douglas McCosh smiled somewhat meekly as he rose to return to his office. "I'll give it a try, sir," he said. His first step was to gather the additional information shown in Exhibit 2.

---

[1]During the past 15 years, several books (e.g., Andrews 1971; Henderson 1979; Porter 1980) as well as articles (e.g., Buzzell et al. 1975; Govindarajan and Gupta 1985) have been published in the field of strategic management. In addition, two new journals (*Strategic Management Journal* and *Journal of Business Strategy*) have been introduced in the strategy area during the past 10 years. Also, traditional management journals such as *Administrative Science Quarterly, Academy of Management Journal,* and *Academy of Management Review* have, during the past decade, started to regularly publish articles on strategy formulation and implementation.

SOURCE: This case is taken from John K. Shank, *Contemporary Management Accounting: A Casebook* (Englewood Cliffs, N. J.: Prentice-Hall, 1981), pp.174–76.

EXHIBIT 1

KINKEAD EQUIPMENT, LTD.
Preliminary Operating Results
January 15, 1979
(thousands of pounds)

		Budget 1978	Percent of Turnover	Actual 1978	Percent of Turnover
Turnover		£6,215	100.0%	£6,319	100.0%
Trading margin		2,590	41.7	2,660	42.1
Less other expenses					
Selling	£706		(11.4)	£740	(11.7)
Administrative	320		(5.1)	325	(5.1)
Research	318	1,344	(5.1)	325	1,390	(5.1)
Profit before taxes		£1,246	20.05%		£1,270	20.10%

Summary for 1978

	Budget	Actual	Variance
Turnover	£6,215	£6,319	104F
Expenses	4,969	5,049	80U
Profit before taxes	£1,246	£1,270	24F

EXHIBIT 2 Additional Information*†

	Electric Meters (EM)‡	Electronic Instruments (EI)‡
Selling prices per unit		
Average standard price	£30.00	£150.00
Average actual prices, 1978	29.00	153.00
Product costs per unit		
Average standard manufacturing cost	15.00	40.00
Average actual manufacturing cost	16.00	42.00
Average standard selling commission	1.00	15.00
Average actual selling commission	.98	14.90
		(continued)

*Kinkead's products are grouped into two main lines of business for internal reporting purposes. Each line includes many separate products, which are averaged together for purposes of this case.

†Kinkead uses a variable costing system for internal reporting purposes.

‡Both EM and EI would be classified as industrial measuring instruments. The two groups serve similar basic functions but differ in their manufacturing technology and their end use characteristics. EM is based on mechanical and electrical technology whereas EI is based on microchip technology. EM and EI are substitute products in the same sense that a mechanical watch and a digital watch are substitutes.

EXHIBIT 2   *(concluded)*

	Electric Meters (EM)‡	Electronic Instruments (EI)‡
Volume information		
Units produced and sold—actual	65,369	28,910
Units produced and sold—planned	82,867	24,860
Total industry turnover, 1978—actual	£26 million	£36 million
Kinkead's share of the market (percent of physical units)		
Planned	10%	10%
Actual	10%	8%

Firm-wide Expenses (thousands of pounds)

	Planned	Actual
Fixed manufacturing expenses	£1,388	£1,399
Fixed selling expenses	250	245
Fixed administrative expenses	320	325
Fixed research expenses	318	325

PHASE I THINKING: THE "ANNUAL REPORT" APPROACH TO VARIANCE ANALYSIS

A straight-forward, simple-minded explanation of the difference between actual profit (£1,270) and the budgeted profit (£1,246) might proceed as follows:

	Plan (£)		Actual (£)	
Sales	6,215		6,319	
Gross margin	2,590	(41.7%)	2,660	(42.1%)
Other Expenses				
Selling	706	(11.4%)	740	(11.7%)
Administrative	320	(5%)	325	(5%)
Research	318	(5%)	325	(5%)
Profit before Tax	£1,246		£1,270	

Incidently, this type of variance analysis is what one usually sees in published annual reports (where the comparison is typically between last year and this year). If we limit ourselves to this type of analysis, we will draw the following conclusions about Kinkead's performance:

Phase I Thinking
Performance Evaluation Summary

- Good sales performance (1 + percent above plan).
- Good manufacturing cost control (margins above plan).
- Selling overspent a bit (slightly up as percent of sales).
- Administration and R&D overspent a bit (but constant as percent of sales).

Overall evaluation: Nothing of major significance; performance essentially on target with profit above plan.

How accurately does the above summary reflect the actual performance of Kinkead? One objective of this chapter is to demonstrate that the above analysis is dangerously inept and very misleading. Part of the reason for this lies in the fact that the plan for 1978 has embedded in it certain expectations about the state of the total industry and about Kinkead's market share, its selling prices, and its cost structure. It is more "actionable" if changes in actual results for 1978 are analyzed against each one of these expectations. The Phase I analysis simply does not break down the overall favorable variance of £24 according to the key underlying causal factors.

PHASE II THINKING: A MANAGEMENT-ORIENTED APPROACH TO VARIANCE ANALYSIS

The analytical framework proposed by Shank and Churchill (1977) to conduct variance analysis—call it Phase II thinking—incorporates the following key ideas:

1. Identify the key causal factors that affect profits.
2. Break down the overall profit variance by these key causal factors.
3. Focus always on the *profit* impact of variation in each causal factor.
4. Try to calculate the specific, separable impact of each causal factor, by varying only that factor while holding all other factors constant ("spinning only one dial at a time").

5. Add complexity sequentially, one layer at a time, beginning at a very basic common-sense level ("peel the onion").

6. Stop the process when the added complexity at a newly created level is not justified by added useful insights into the causal factors underlying the overall profit variance.

Exhibits 6–1 and 6–2 contain the explanation for the overall favorable profit variance of £24 using the above approach. In the interest of brevity, most of the calculational details are suppressed (detailed calculations are available from the authors).

What can we say about the performance of Kinkead if we now consider the variance analysis summarized in Exhibit 6–2? The following insights can be offered:

Phase II Thinking
Performance Evaluation Summary

Functional Areas	Comments		Overall Evaluation
Marketing	Market share (SOM) decline cost the firm	£229U	Good performance
	But, fortunately, sales mix was managed toward the higher margin products	579F	
	Net	£350F	
	Uncontrollables: Unfortunately, the overall market declined and cost the firm	£210U	
Manufacturing	Poor manufacturing cost control cost the firm (65 + 58 + 11)	£134U	Poor performance
R&D	R&D budget overspent a bit	£7U	Satisfactory performance
Administration	Administration budget overspent a bit	£5U	Satisfactory performance

Thus, the overall evaluation of the general manager would probably be satisfactory, though there are specific areas (such as manufacturing cost control or share of market) that need attention. The above summary is quite different—and clearly superior—to the one presented under Phase I thinking. But, can we do better? We believe that Shank and Churchill's framework needs to be modified in important ways to accommodate the following ideas:

1. Sales volume, share of market, and sales mix variances are calculated on the presumption that Kinkead is essentially a single product firm with two different varieties of the product. This means that the target customers for EM and EI are the same and that they view the two products as substitutable. Is Kinkead a single product firm with two product offerings, or does the firm compete in two different markets? In other words, does Kinkead have a single strategy for EM and EI or does the firm have two strategies for the two businesses? As we argue later, EM and EI have very different industry characteristics and compete in very different markets, thereby requiring quite different strategies. It is, therefore, more useful to calculate market size and market share variances separately for EM and EI. Just introducing the concept of a *sales mix* variance implies that the average standard profit contribution across EM and EI together is meaningful.

For an ice cream manufacturer, for example, it is probably reasonable to assume that the firm operates in a single industry with multiple product offerings, all targeted at the same customer group. It would, therefore, be meaningful to calculate a sales mix variance since vanilla ice cream and strawberry ice cream, for instance, are substitutable and more sales of one implies less sales of the other for the firm (for an elaboration on these ideas, refer to the Midwest Ice Cream Company case, 1982). On the other hand, for a firm such as General Electric, it is much less clear whether a sales mix variance across jet engines, steam turbines, and light bulbs really makes any sense. This is more nearly the case for Kinkead since one unit of EM (which costs £29) is not really fully substitutable for one unit of EI (which costs £153).

An important issue in the history of many industries is to determine when product differentiation has progressed sufficiently that what *was* a single business with two varieties *is now* two businesses. Some examples include the growth of the electronic cash register for NCR, the growth of the digital watch for Bulova, or the growth of the industrial robot for General Electric.

2. Performance evaluation (in Phase II thinking) did not relate the variances to the differing strategic contexts facing EM and EI.

EXHIBIT 6–1 Variance Calculations Using Shank and Churchill's Management-Oriented Framework

| | Plan | Key Causal Factors | | | | Actual |
	1	2	3	4	5	6
Total market	Expected	Actual	Actual	Actual	Actual	Actual
Market share	Expected	Expected	Actual	Actual	Actual	Actual
Sales mix	Expected	Expected	Expected	Actual	Actual	Actual
Selling price	Expected	Expected	Expected	Expected	Actual	Actual
Costs	Expected	Expected	Expected	Expected	Expected	Actual
Sales	£6,215	5,847	5,440	6,298	6,319	6,319
Variable costs	£2,693	2,535	2,357	2,636	2,636	2,755
Contribution	£3,522	3,312	3,083	3,662	3,683	3,564

Fixed costs	£2,276	2,276	2,276	2,276	2,276	2,294
Profit	£1,246	1,036	807	1,386	1,407	1,270

Level "1" — Overall variance £24F

Level "2" — Sales volume and mix £140F   Sales prices and costs £116U

Level "3"
- Sales volume £439U
- Sales mix £579F
- Sales prices £21F
- Costs £137U

Level "4"
- Market size £210U
- Market share £229U

Sales mix £579F:
- EM £1,222U
- EI £1,801F

Sales prices £21F:
- EM £65U
- EI £86F

Variable costs
- Manufacturing EM £65U / EI £58U
- Selling commission EM £1F / EI £3F

Fixed costs
- Manufacturing £11U
- Selling £5F
- Administration £5U
- R&D £7U

EXHIBIT 6–2   Variance Summary for the Phase II Approach

Overall market decline	£210(U)
Share of market decline	229(U)

Sales mix change
    EM £1,222(U)
    EI £1,801(F)
	579(F)

Sales prices improved
    EM £65(U)
    EI £86(F)
	21(F)

Manufacturing cost control
    Variable costs £123(U)
    Fixed costs £11(U)
	134(U)

Other
    R&D £7(U)
    Administration £5(U)
    Sales commission £4(F)
    Selling cost £5(F)
	3(U)

Total	£ 24(F)

PHASE III THINKING: VARIANCE ANALYSIS USING A STRATEGIC FRAMEWORK

We argue that performance evaluation—which is a critical component of the management control process—needs to be tailored to the strategy being followed by a firm or its business units. We offer the following set of arguments in support of our position: (1) Different strategies imply different tasks and require different behaviors for effective performance (Andrews 1971; Gupta and Govindarajan 1984a); (2) Different control systems induce different behaviors (Gupta and Govindarajan 1984b); (3) Thus, superior performance can best be achieved by tailoring control systems to the requirements of particular strategies.[2]

We will first define and briefly elaborate the concept of strategy before illustrating how to link strategic considerations with variances for management control and evaluation. Strategy has been conceptualized by

---

[2]Several studies have shown that when an individual's rewards are tied to performance along certain dimensions, his/her behavior would be guided by the desire to optimize performance with respect to those dimensions. Refer to Govindarajan and Gupta (1985) for a review of these studies.

Andrews (1971), Ansoff (1965), Chandler (1962), Hofer and Schendel (1978), Miles and Snow (1978), and others as the process by which managers, using a three- to five-year time horizon, evaluate external environmental opportunities as well as internal strengths and resources in order to decide on *goals* as well as *a set of action plans* to accomplish these goals. Thus, a business unit's (or a firm's) strategy depends upon two interrelated aspects: (1) its strategic mission or goals and (2) the way the business unit chooses to compete in its industry to accomplish its goals—the business unit's competitive strategy.

Turning first to strategic mission, consulting firms such as Boston Consulting Group (Henderson 1978), Arthur D. Little (Wright 1975), and A.T. Kearney (Hofer and Davoust 1977) as well as academic researchers such as Buzzell and Wiersema (1981) and Hofer and Schendel (1978) have proposed the following three strategic missions that a business unit can adopt:

Build.   This mission implies a goal of increased market share, even at the expense of short-term earnings and cash flow. A business unit following this mission is expected to be a net user of cash in that the cash throwoff from its current operations would usually be insufficient to meet its capital investment needs. Business units with "low market share" in "high growth industries" typically pursue a "build" mission (e.g., Apple Computer's MacIntosh business, Monsanto's Biotechnology business).

Hold.   This strategic mission is geared to the protection of the business unit's market share and competitive position. The cash outflows for a business unit following this mission would usually be more or less equal to cash inflows. Businesses with "high market share" in "high growth industries" typically pursue a "hold" mission (e.g., IBM in mainframe computers).

Harvest.   This mission implies a goal of maximizing short-term earnings and cash flow, even at the expense of market share. A business unit following such a mission would be a net supplier of cash. Businesses with "high market share" in "low growth industries" typically pursue a "harvest" mission (e.g., American Brands in tobacco products).

In terms of competitive strategy, Porter (1980) has proposed the following two generic ways in which businesses can develop sustainable competitive advantage:

Low Cost.   The primary focus of this strategy is to achieve low cost relative to competitors. Cost leadership can be achieved through approaches such as economies of scale in production, learning curve effects, tight cost control, and cost minimization in areas such as R&D, service, sales force, or advertising. Examples of firms following this strategy include: Texas Instruments in consumer electronics, Emerson Electric in electric motors, Chevrolet in automobiles, Briggs and Stratton in gasoline engines, Black and Decker in machine tools, and Commodore in business machines.

Differentiation.   The primary focus of this strategy is to differentiate the product offering of the business unit, creating something that is perceived by customers as being unique. Approaches to product differentiation include: brand loyalty (Coca-Cola in soft drinks), superior customer service (IBM in computers), dealer network (Caterpillar Tractors in construction equipment), product design and product features (Hewlett-Packard in electronics), and/or product technology (Coleman in camping equipment).

The above framework allows us to explicitly consider the strategic positioning of the two product groups—Electric Meters and Electronic Instruments. Though they both are industrial measuring instruments, they face very different competitive conditions which very probably call for different strategies. Exhibit 6–3 summarizes the differing environments and the resulting strategic issues.

How well did Electric Meters and Electronic Instruments perform, given their strategic contexts? The relevant variance calculations are given in Exhibits 6–4 and 6–5. These calculations differ from Phase II analysis (given in Exhibit 6–1) in one important respect. Exhibit 6–1 treated EM and EI as two varieties of one product, competing as substitutes, with a single strategy. Thus, a sales mix variance was computed. Exhibits 6–4 and 6–5 treat EM and EI as different products with dissimilar strategies. Therefore, there is no attempt to calculate a sales mix variance. The basic idea is that even though a sales mix variance can always be calculated, the concept is only meaningful when a single business framework is applicable. For the same reason, Exhibits 6–4 and 6–5 report the market size and market share variances for EM and EI separately, while Exhibit 6–1 reported these two variances for the instruments business as a whole. Obviously there is a high degree of subjectivity involved in deciding whether Kinkead is in one business or two. The fact that the judgment is to a large extent subjective does not negate its importance.

EXHIBIT 6–3   Strategic Contexts of the Two Businesses

		Electric Meters	*Electronic Instruments*
Overall market	Plan	828,670	248,600
(units):	Actual	653,690	361,375
		Declining market (22% decrease)	Growth Market (45% increase)
Kinkead's share:	Plan	10%	10%
	Actual	10%	8%

EXHIBIT 6–3   (*concluded*)

		Electric Meters	Electronic Instruments
Kinkead's prices:	Plan	£30	£150
	Actual	£29	£153
		We apparently cut price to hold share	We apparently raised price to ration the high demand
Kinkead's margin:	Plan	£14	£95
	Actual	£12	£96
Industry prices:	Actual	£40	£99
		We are well below "market"	We are well above "market"
Selling commission		3% of sales	10% of sales
Product/market characteristics		Mature Lower technology Declining market Lower margins Low unit price Industry prices holding up Low commissions	Evolving Higher technology Growth market Higher margins High unit price Industry prices falling rapidly High commissions
Kinkead's apparent strategic mission		"Hold"	"Skim" or "Harvest"
Kinkead's apparent competitive strategy		The low price implies we are trying for low cost position	The high price implies we are trying for a differentiation position
A more plausible strategy		"Harvest"	"Build"
Key success factors (arising from the plausible strategy)		Hold sales prices vis-à-vis competition Do not focus on maintaining and improving SOM Aggressive cost control Process R&D to reduce unit costs	Competitively price to gain SOM Product R&D Lower costs through experience curve effects

EXHIBIT 6–4   Variance Calculations Using a Strategic Framework

Key Causal Factors	(1) Plan	(2)	(3)	(4)	(5) Actual
Total market	Expected	Actual	Actual	Actual	Actual
Market share	Expected	Expected	Actual	Actual	Actual
Selling price	Expected	Expected	Expected	Actual	Actual
Variable costs	Expected	Expected	Expected	Expected	Actual

Electric meters

Sales	£2,486	£1,961	£1,961	£1,896	£1,896
Variable costs	1,326	1,046	1,046	1,046	1,110
Contribution	£1,160	£ 915	£ 915	£ 850	£ 786

Market size £245(U)   Market share –0–   Sales price £65(U)   Variable cost £64(U)

Mfg. £65(U)   Selling £1F

Electronic Instruments

Sales	£3,729	£5,421	£4,337	£4,423	£4,423
Variable costs	1,367	1,988	1,590	1,590	1,645
Contribution	£2,362	£3,433	£2,747	£2,833	£2,778

Market size £1,071(F)   Market share £686(U)   Sales price £86(F)   Variable cost £55(U)

Mfg. £58(U)   Selling £3F

Firmwide fixed costs (by responsibility centers)

	Budget	Actual	Variance
Manufacturing	£1,388	£1,399	£11U
Selling	250	245	5F
Administration	320	325	5U
R&D	318	325	7U

EXHIBIT 6–5   Variance Summary for the Phase III Approach

Electric Meters	
Market size	£ 245(U)
Market share	–0–
Sales price	65(U)
Variable manufacturing cost	65(U)
Selling commission	1(F)
Electronic instruments	
Market size	1,071(F)
Market share	686(U)
Sales price	86(F)
Variable manufacturing cost	58(U)
Selling commission	3(F)
Firmwide fixed costs	
Manufacturing	11(U)
Selling	5(F)
Administration	5(U)
R&D	7(U)
Total	£ 24(F)

The following table summarizes the managerial performance evaluation that would result if we were to evaluate EM and EI against their plausible strategies, using the variances reported in Exhibits 6–4 and 6–5.

The overall performance of Kinkead would probably be judged as "unsatisfactory." The firm has not taken appropriate decisions in its functional areas—marketing, manufacturing, R&D, and administration—either for its harvest business (EM) or for its build business (EI). This summary indicates a dramatically different picture of Kinkead's performance than the one discussed under Phase II thinking. This is to be expected since Phase II thinking did not tie variance analysis to strategic objectives. Neither Phase I nor Phase II analyses explicitly focused on ways to improve performance en route to accomplishing strategic goals. This would then imply that rewards ought not to be tied to performance assessment undertaken using Phase I or Phase II frameworks. Yet, Phase II analysis represents the best current thinking on variance analysis—at least as documented in the literature!

Phase III Thinking
Performance Evaluation Summary

Functional Areas	Electric Meters "Harvest" versus "Hold"		Electronic Instruments "Build" versus "Skim"	
	Comments	*Overall Evaluation*	*Comments*	*Overall Evaluation*
Marketing	If we had held prices and share, decline in this mature business would have cost us £245U	Poor performance	We raised prices to maintain margins and to ration our scarce capacity (our price was £153 versus the industry price of £99).	Poor performance
	But, we were further hurt by price cuts made in order to hold our SOM (our price was £29 versus the industry price of £40) 65U Net £310U		In the process, we lost ⅕th of our SOM which cost us (netted against £87F from sales prices) £600U	
	This is a market which declined 22 percent. Why are we sacrificing margins to hold market position in this mature, declining, lower margin business.		This is a booming market which grew 45 percent during this period. Then, why did we decide to improve margins at the expense of SOM in this fast growing, higher margin business?	
	We underspent the selling cost budget (1 + 5) £6F		Fortunately, growth in the total market improved our profit picture £1,071F	
	But, why are we cutting back here in the face of our major marketing problems?		We underspent the selling cost budget (3 + 5) £8F	

Area	Comments / Questions	Assessment
Manufacturing	Manufacturing cost control was lousy and cost the firm (65 + 11) £76U	Poor performance
	If we are trying to be a cost leader, where are the benefits of our cumulative experience or our scale economies?	
	But, why are we cutting back here in the face of our major marketing problems?	
	Variable manufacturing costs showed an unfavorable variance of £58U.	Poor performance
	Does the higher manufacturing cost result in a product perceived as better?	
	Apparently not, based on share data.	
R&D	Why did manufacturing costs not go down as a result of overspending the R&D budget?	Poor performance
	If this is process R&D, it isn't working. If it is product R&D, where are the results?	Poor performance
Administration	Inadequate control over overhead costs, given the need to become the low cost producer.	Poor performance
	Administration budget overspent a bit (£5U).	Not satisfactory
	How does this relate to cost control?	

CONCLUSIONS

Variance analysis represents a key link in the management control process. It involves two steps. First, one needs to break down the overall profit variance by key causal factors. Second, one needs to put the pieces back together most meaningfully with a view to evaluating managerial performance. Putting the bits and pieces together most meaningfully is just as crucial as computing the pieces. This is a managerial function, not a calculational one.

Phase I, Phase II, and Phase III thinking yield different implications for this first step. That is, the detailed variance calculations do differ across the three approaches. Their implications differ even more for the second step. The calculational aspects identify the variance as either favorable or unfavorable. However, a favorable variance does not necessarily imply favorable performance; similarly, an unfavorable variance does not necessarily imply unfavorable performance. We argue that the link between a favorable or unfavorable variance, on the one hand, and favorable or unfavorable performance, on the other, depends upon the strategic context of the business under evaluation.

No doubt, judgments about managerial performance can be dramatically different under Phase I, Phase II, and Phase III thinking (as the Kinkead case illustrates). In our view, moving toward the third generation thinking (i.e., analyzing profit variances in terms of the strategic issues involved) represents progress in adapting *cost analysis* to the new era in which *strategic analysis* is a major element in business thinking.

DISCUSSION QUESTIONS

1. Focus your attention on Exhibits 6–1 and 6–2. What can you say about the performance of Kinkead based on these exhibits?
2. Now, focus on Exhibits 6–3, 6–4, and 6–5. What can you say about the performance of Kinkead based on these exhibits?
3. You are asked to decide the incentive bonus for Manufacturing, Marketing, and R&D managers of Kinkead. What would be your decisions? Why?
4. What strategic cost analysis ideas can you identify based on the Kinkead case? Are they generalizable?

REFERENCES

Andrews, K. R. *The Concept of Corporate Strategy.* Homewood, Ill.: Dow Jones-Irwin, 1971.

Ansoff, H. I. *Corporate Strategy.* New York: McGraw-Hill, 1965.

Buzzell, R. D.; G. Bradley; and R. G. M. Sultan. "Market Share—A Key to Profitability." *Harvard Business Review* 53, January–February 1975, pp. 97–106.

Buzzell, R. D., and F. D. Wiersema. "Modelling Changes in Market Share: A Cross-Sectional Analysis." *Strategic Management Journal* 2, 1981, pp. 27–42.

Chandler, A. D. *Strategy and Structure*. Cambridge, Mass.: The MIT Press, 1962.

Govindarajan, V., and A. K. Gupta. "Linking Control Systems to Business Unit Strategy: Impact on Performance." *Accounting, Organizations and Society* 10, no. 1, 1985, pp. 51–66.

Gupta, A. K., and V. Govindarajan. "Business Unit Strategy, Managerial Characteristics, and Business Unit Effectiveness at Strategy Implementation." *Academy of Management Journal* 27, 1984a, pp. 25–41.

————. "Build, Hold, Harvest: Converting Strategic Intentions into Reality." *Journal of Business Strategy* 4, no. 3, 1984b, pp. 34–47.

Henderson, B. D. *Henderson on Corporate Strategy*. Cambridge, Mass.: Abt Books, 1978.

Hofer, C. W., and M. J. Davoust. *Successful Strategic Management*. Chicago, Ill.: A.T. Kearney, Inc., 1977.

Hofer, C. W., and D. E. Schendel. *Strategy Formulation: Analytical Concepts*. St. Paul, Minn.: West Publishing, 1978.

Miles, R. E., and C. C. Snow. *Organizational Strategy, Structure and Process*. New York: McGraw-Hill, 1978.

Porter, M. E. *Competitive Strategy*. New York: Free Press, 1980.

Shank, J. K. "Midwest Ice Cream Company," in *Contemporary Management Accounting: A Casebook*. Englewood Cliffs, N.J.: Prentice-Hall, 1982, pp. 157–73.

————. *Contemporary Management Accounting: A Casebook*. Englewood Cliffs, N.J.: Prentice-Hall, 1981.

Shank, J. K., and N. C. Churchill. "Variance Analysis: A Management-Oriented Approach." *The Accounting Review*, October 1977, pp. 950–57.

Wright, R. V. L. *A System for Managing Diversity*. Cambridge, Mass.: Arthur D. Little, Inc., 1975.

CHAPTER 7

The Trubrite Dyes Case— Differentiating Cost Analysis and Control Depending on the Strategy Being Followed*

This chapter presents a live (but disguised) case to illustrate two key ideas in strategically based cost analysis and control. The case is part of the effort to adapt the traditional body of knowledge called cost analysis to the rapidly developing body of knowledge on strategy formulation and implementation. The primary rationale for cost analysis has always been decision relevance, as evidenced by the well-worn catch phrase "relevant cost analysis." As thinking evolves about the strategy formulation and implementation process, relevant cost analysis must take strategic analysis more fully into account. This is a new thrust in managerial accounting, but one which is likely to receive increased attention in the future.

In particular, this case illustrates two ideas: (1) The use of cost analysis to identify the differing strategic positions of three products of a large chemicals manufacturer and (2) the use of differentiated management controls focusing on the differing key success factors for the differentiated strategies for the three products.

---

* A modified version of this chapter appeared in the *Journal of Cost Management*, Fall 1988. Reproduced with permission.

MONARCH CHEMICALS—THE TRUBRITE
DYEING SYSTEM

Textile Dyestuffs

Textile manufacturing, viewed in aggregate, is a well known example of an American industry that is well past its prime. Once known in world markets for product dominance, manufacturing innovations, cost and price leadership, and substantial profits, the industry is now growing at less than 1 percent per year, is only marginally profitable, and is operating substantially below capacity. Foreign competition continues to erode the markets for U. S.-produced textile products. Nevertheless, the industry is still huge, accounting for 700,000 jobs and $51 billion in sales in 1983. Monarch Chemical is a leading firm in dyestuffs sold to domestic textile manufacturers.

Monarch, a broad-based chemicals manufacturer, had considered divestiture of its entire dyestuffs business as recently as 1980 because of the obsolescent technologies used, the vast industry overcapacity, the severe price competition, the limited profitability, the possibility of latent toxicology problems, and the fact that Monarch did not have sufficient strength in any segment of the industry. Long-run viability required the development either of a product leadership position or a cost leadership position in selected segments as a basis for building sales volumes large enough to generate an acceptable return on the invested capital. Rather than divest the U.S. business, Monarch made the commitment in 1981 to become the low cost producer in selected segments to permit capturing leading sales volume positions. Two major positive features of the dyestuffs business are that the product is essential in textile manufacturing (no substitutes) and is a small factor in final product cost (only a few cents per square yard of fabric). The goal for dyestuffs was cash generation for investment in other, more dynamic, businesses. This case concerns the firm's programs to achieve acceptable profitability in one segment of the dyestuffs business which is still experiencing at least modest growth, Trubrite fabric dyes.

Trubrite Dyes

In 1976, Monarch had introduced a new system of fabric dyeing in the product niches it served. The new system used a dramatically different chemical formulation which was patentable. Other firms had collab-

SOURCE: This case was made possible by the cooperation of a major multinational firm which prefers to remain anonymous.

orated with Monarch in parts of the research and thus were included in some of the patents. This new system was given the brand name *Trubrite* by Monarch. The Trubrite dyes not only exhibited much better color "fastness," but were also technologically superior in terms of *diffusion* rate, *migration* rate, *absorption* rate, and *solubility,* all very important features to textiles manufacturers.

All shades of fabric color are achieved by blending appropriate proportions of the three primary color dyes; red, blue, and yellow. The new Trubrite dye system worked best when all three Trubrite dyes were used together. This presented a dramatic opportunity to sell manufacturers all of the dyestuff required for all three blending colors instead of selling each color separately as had been the practice in the past. Because Trubrite was such a major technological innovation, it achieved widespread market acceptance even though Monarch priced the Trubrite three-color system at more than twice the prices for competing dyes. As a result, the achieved margins for the new dyes were very high initially.

All manufacturing of Trubrite dyes was done in one plant which was among the largest dyestuffs manufacturing facilities in the United States. This plant had been built in 1956 as a joint venture of three chemical firms, Monarch, Trojan, and Ajax.

Yellow Trubrite Dye.   Over the late 1970s, Yellow Trubrite (Yellow TB) dye accounted for a steady 65 percent of total sales of yellow dye to customers in this niche. All three of the joint venture partners, Monarch, Ajax, and Trojan, shared rights to the Yellow TB dye. Thus, all three were selling an identical product produced at the same factory and purchased at the same price. Monarch had about one half of this business originally. However, by the end of 1980, price cutting by both Ajax and Trojan had reduced Monarch's penetration to about 25 percent of the business and the downward trend was continuing.

Early in 1981, Monarch undertook a special "blitz" sales campaign, offering customers who would sign up immediately for a one-year contract a price of $5.50 per pound versus its previous price of $6.50 (competitors were at about $6.00). Monarch gained a 68 percent share of the business with this ploy which took the competitors completely by surprise. A few months later Monarch announced that it had bought out Ajax and Trojan from the joint venture manufacturing plant. This plant then became Monarch's only dyestuffs plant. Ajax gave up on the yellow fabric dyes business soon thereafter. After the one-year contracts expired, Trojan moved aggressively to regain the business it had lost. In 1982, Trojan began to manufacture yellow fabric dye at its own facility, a newly constructed plant in which, presumably, they also were trying to achieve cost leadership via large volumes. By 1983, the yellow fabric dye business had become primarily a two competitor race with Trojan and Monarch both using price very aggressively and each possessing about 50 percent of the business. Data on price, volumes, and profitability for this segment between 1976 and 1983 are summarized in Exhibit 1 below:

EXHIBIT 1   Yellow Dye

	Industry Volume (000 lbs.)	Monarch Volume (000 lbs.)	Monarch Share (Percent)	Monarch Selling Price (per lb.)	Monarch Variable Cost (per lb.)
1976	225	113	50%	$7.14	$3.00
1977	310	154	50	7.58	2.72
1978	500	251	50	8.00	2.80
1979	880	353	40	7.48	2.62
1980	1,850	554	30	6.96	3.20
1981	2,214	443*/920	20*/42	6.30*/5.50	3.48
1982	2,065	1,164	56	4.40	3.70
1983	2,637	1,285	49	4.24	3.30

*The numbers above the diagonal for 1981 represent the projected figures for the year if price had not been cut at midyear. The numbers below the diagonal are the actual numbers for the year reflecting the price cuts at midyear. In the fourth quarter of 1981, penetration actually achieved a 68 percent figure.

Blue Trubrite Dye.   The market for blue fabric dye is split depending on whether or not sensitivity to light is important. For that portion of the business for which this feature is not important Monarch is not a factor. For the major and growing portion of the business for which light sensitivity is important the major competitors have been Monarch, Ajax, and Spartan. Between 1976 and 1981, Monarch and Ajax shared the rights to Blue TB and thus were selling exactly the same product manufactured at the same (joint venture) plant. Trojan, the third partner in this plant, had not chosen to compete in the blue dyes business because of patent access complications. The Spartan product (Blue 79) is similar to Blue TB, but somewhat lower in quality. Also, its patent protection is not as secure. Blue 79 is somewhat cheaper to produce (about 10 percent less than Blue TB). Through 1980, Blue TB captured about half the business and Blue 79 about half. Monarch and Ajax were roughly comparable on price for Blue TB ($19 per lb.) and Spartan was about $1 below for Blue 79 ($18 per lb.). When Monarch acquired Ajax's share of the joint venture factory in 1981, Monarch was confident that Ajax was dropping out of the Blue

TB business. Monarch decided to follow a strategy of meeting Spartan's prices in the marketplace head-on, trying to push technical superiority to achieve 60 percent penetration. In late 1981 Monarch cut price to $18 per lb. to meet the Blue 79 price. Spartan nudged price a little below $18 and the two-way struggle seemed to be underway, but still at a profitable price level. Then the roof fell in!

Ajax, which had lost out to Monarch in the yellow dye business in 1981, did not drop out of the blue dye business when it sold its share of the joint venture manufacturing plant. Instead, it took advantage of the softer patent protection on Blue 79 to begin manufacturing it at another plant. To take away Blue 79 business from Spartan, Ajax used very aggressive price cuts. They cut the price to $14.50 per pound in late 1981, but Spartan matched them. At this point, Monarch held Blue TB at $18. By 1983, Ajax had cut Blue 79 all the way to $9 per lb. and Spartan had followed. Monarch had cut Blue TB to $16.40 per lb. by 1983. From a 49 percent penetration in 1981, Trubrite Blue had dropped all the way to 22 percent in 1983. Blue TB sales volume was stable and even growing somewhat, but the much lower price for Blue 79 had generated dramatic sales growth in which Monarch was not sharing. At these lower prices, users who don't require the light sensitivity feature began switching to the light sensitive segment anyway. Everyone likes this feature even though it is not critical in all applications. At a low enough price, even those who don't require it will buy it. Data on price, volumes, and profitability for this segment for 1981–1983 are summarized in Exhibit 2.

Red Trubrite Dye.   Trubrite is the clearly superior red product for fabric dyeing. The patents are owned separately by Monarch so neither Trojan nor Ajax had ever had access to red dye manufacturing at the joint venture plant. Up through 1982, Red TB was the high price, high quality, high margin, leading product in this business segment.

The main difficulty with Red TB stems from a change in dyeing technology which has been underway since the late 1970s. By 1983, only

EXHIBIT 2   Blue Dye (light sensitive segment only)

	Industry Volume (000 lbs.)	Monarch Volume (000 lbs.)	Monarch Share (Percent)	Monarch Selling Price (per lb.)	Ajax Selling Price (per lb.)	Monarch Variable Cost (per lb.)
1981	907	449	49%	$18.00	$14.50	$6.04
1982	1,322	476	36	16.60	11.00	6.06
1983	2,586	573	22	16.40	9.00	7.22

about 30 percent of fabric in the relevant niche was still being dyed by *batch* processing. *Continuous* spray dyeing machines were used for 70 percent of the applications. It was believed in the industry that batch dyeing would remain the preferred method for perhaps 25 percent of the fabric sold. The continuous spray-dyeing machines operate at much lower temperatures. They substitute pressurized spraying for *cooking* as the way to fully impregnate the fabric with the dye. At these lower temperatures, the technical superiority of the Trubrite Red dye is not achieved. Not only are competing products such as Red 66 dye technically comparable in the "cold spray" continuous dyeing machines, they also were priced much lower ($6.60 per lb. in October of 1983 versus $16.70 for Red TB). Even more troublesome was a new Red dye (Red XL) introduced by Spartan in 1983 which seemed to be not just equal but actually technically superior to Red TB in some lower temperature continuous spray dyeing applications. Spartan appeared to be willing to stay close to Monarch's "price umbrella," as they had for blue dyes. They introduced this new Red XL at a $16 price per pound. This was still $.70 below the price of Red TB, however.

Trubrite Red was still the leading product for both batch and continuous dyeing applications in late 1983 with more than 40 percent penetration. In fact, Monarch had successfully defended patent infringement suits against both Ajax and Spartan for Red TB, indicating the superiority of this product. However, its penetration was beginning to erode for the continuous applications. A new technology using high-temperature-spray dyeing (gaining the joint benefits of heat and pressure) was emerging in 1983. This process could reassert the technical superiority of Red TB, were it to gain acceptance. Monarch, in fact, was experimenting with a hot spray dyeing process in its research labs. Equipment manufacturers were also touting new hot spray processes. It thus was not clear that Red TB was in a state of decline. However, implementing a strategy of high volume to achieve cost leadership suggested that pricing for Red TB needed to be carefully evaluated. Complicating this picture was the fact that *lower* prices did not necessarily move the short run price-volume-profitability trade-off in the direction of *higher* distributable cash generation for a product. Price, volume, and profitability data for red fabric dyes for 1981–83 are summarized in Exhibit 3.

Trubrite Manufacturing Costs

Another factor to consider in pricing the Trubrite dyes was manufacturing cost performance. In 1983 Monarch's only dyestuffs plant (though fully utilized) was very inefficient by modern standards. Most of the equipment was more than 20 years old. Even though it was generally well maintained, the basic production process had not changed since 1956, and

EXHIBIT 3 Red Dye

	Industry Volume (000 lbs.)	Monarch Volume (000 lbs.)	Monarch Share (Percent)	Monarch Selling Price	Red 66 Selling Price	Red XL Selling Price	Monarch Variable Cost
1981	2,053	732	36%	$17.50	$8.00	$ —	$5.22
1982	1,914	867	45	16.60	7.80	—	5.78
1983	2,409	1,036	43	16.70	6.60	16.00	6.14

EXHIBIT 4   Trubrite Products Costs (dollars per lb.)

	Yellow		Blue		Red	
	V/C	T/C	V/C	T/C	V/C	T/C
1981	$3.48	$5.28	$6.04	$17.02	$5.22	$8.96
1982	3.70	5.72	6.06	14.52	5.78	9.20
1983	3.30	4.94	7.22	10.00	6.14	8.40

was out of date. During 1983, however, a major consolidation, renovation, and modernization program was initiated which was designed to improve yields substantially, to double the output per equipment hour, to cut labor costs dramatically, and to reduce inventory levels significantly. Overall, this program involved a time-phased expenditure of $35 million to generate $14 million per year in savings by 1985. It was felt that this program would give Monarch a cost leadership edge for approximately 4 to 7 years, and perhaps for 8 to 10 years if competitors did not react quickly and could not match the inherent advantages from the large size of Monarch's plant. Still, it had to be acknowledged that the plant was never going to overcome the cost problems typical of any multipurpose chemicals factory. In 1983 the plant produced and sold 400 different compounds using 100 different basic chemicals drawn from 25 different chemical reaction types. Also, costing individual products was made very difficult by the fact that two thirds of manufacturing cost (excluding raw material) was joint across the entire product line.

Cost data for the three major Trubrite dyes for 1981–83 are summarized in Exhibit 4. Variable product cost data (V/C) were already shown in earlier exhibits. The total cost data (T/C) add on a share of fixed manufacturing expenses allocated on a machine hours basis.

ANALYSIS OF THE CASE

As noted earlier, this case reflects a new thrust in managerial accounting; what we call *strategic cost analysis*. This is something old and something new. The *old* is cost/volume/profit analysis and product profitability assessment. The *new* is a decision setting where the financial analysis must be considered explicitly in the context of the strategy being followed. The analysis considers the appropriateness of that strategy from a financial perspective. This is either financial analysis from a strategic perspective or strategic assessment from a financial perspective—take your choice. The specific decision setting is ostensibly pricing, but product-related development expenditures, capital investment, and performance evaluation and control also are at issue.

The case differs from conventional "relevant cost analysis" situations primarily in terms of the richness of the strategic context. The intent is to provide a case which allows the cost analysis to be imbedded in a strategic analysis which influences the cost analysis in a major way. The particular business (technologically innovative textile dyestuffs) is moving from "high perceived product differentiation/low price sensitivity" toward lower differentiation and higher price sensitivity (Kiechel 1981). Such "drift" is very common for products which are big winners when introduced, but which begin to lose their luster over time. Even though the case looks at one product line, three distinct and different niches are present. In the case of the yellow dye, there are two competitors manufacturing an identical product and competing agressively on price. Thus, yellow dye can easily be deemed a commodity. The blue and red dyes are protected by patents and thus are still differentiated products to some extent. Blue has a close substitute which is priced much lower, but red does not (at least so far). The role of cost analysis and management control are very different for these three different situations.

Strategic Cost Analysis

Profit contribution and full cost profit for the three Trubrite dyes can be calculated from the information in Exhibits 1 through 4. The results are summarized in Exhibit 7–1 below:

EXHIBIT 7–1a   Profit Contribution for Trubrite Dyes (per unit)

	Current Sales Price	−	Variable Mfg. Cost	−	Variable Sales Expense*	=	Profit Contribution
Yellow	$ 4.24		$3.30		$0.26		$ .68
Blue	16.40		7.22		.26		8.92
Red	16.70		6.14		.26		10.30

*In addition to variable manufacturing expenses, a total of $760,000 was incurred in sales commissions paid to a common sales force dealing with the Trubrite line (commissions based on the number of lbs. sold).

Volume = 1,285K + 573K + 1,036K = 2,894K
Cost per pound = $760,000/2,894,000 = $ .26

EXHIBIT 7–1b   Full Cost Profit for Trubrite Dyes (in millions of dollars)

	Sales	Variable Costs	Variable Sales Expense	Fixed Mfg. Expense	Profit
Yellow	$ 5.4	$ (4.2)	$(.34)	$(2.1)	$ (1.24)
Blue	9.4	(4.1)	(.15)	(1.6)	3.55
Red	17.3	(6.4)	(.27)	(2.3)	8.33
Total	$32.1	$(14.7)	$(.76)	$(6.0)	$ 10.64

Exhibits 1, 2, and 3 provide some evidence of how volume might move as price moves. There is strong indication for yellow dye that Trojan would meet any price cut so that no major volume gain would result. "Leading" price backup would enhance profitability only if Trojan would follow, which seems unlikely, given the history. Yellow dye seems to be priced to get high volume but with no net profit to show for the efforts. Since the factory is now operating at capacity, a good question could be raised as to why any capacity at all is being allocated to a marginal profit producer like yellow. Whether Monarch could drop yellow is a good question, regardless of whether they should do so. A three-color-system perspective says you must carry all three colors. But, Monarch is the only firm competing in all three colors now. Yellow is a clear candidate for cost reduction if it is to stay as a profitable product, especially since the competitor—Trojan—has the newer plant. We'll come back to the cost issue later.

Blue dye is an excellent example of cost-volume-profit dynamics. We have very high profit contribution (P/C) per unit ($8.92) and a sizable and modestly growing sales volume. The competing product is priced at about 50 percent of our price and has grown in volume from 458,000 pounds in 1981 to 2,013,000 pounds in 1983. This is roughly 100 percent annual growth for two years! A very large share of the users who were buying non-light-sensitive blue dye when the light sensitive price was $14 to $18 per pound are now willing to buy light sensitive dye when the price is below $10 per pound. The competing product costs about $5.40 per pound to produce (variable cost only, based on 90 percent of our 1982 cost). If we matched the competitor's price we would still have profit contribution of $1.52 per pound (9.00 − 7.48). Since our product is superior, we should get some of their volume. In fact, we had about one half the total volume as recently as 1981, just before the big price cuts on Blue 79. Why are we allowing all this volume to go to the competitors???

The following comparison is a good example of how higher volume is not always preferable in terms of profit contribution. Chasing the extra volume with deep price cuts would actually *reduce* profit substantially in the short run!

Our Price	Our P/C	Our Volume	Total P/C
$16.40	$ 8.92	573K	$5,110K
9.00	1.52	1,293K (50% share?)	1,966K

Monarch feels it isn't wise to try to compete on a price basis with a lower quality product which is cheaper to make. Given this view, why was price cut *at all* in 1982 and 1983? A better idea now might be to raise price back toward $18 to see if volume holds. The price sensitive volume has already shifted to Blue 79. The remaining volume is the quality conscious, price inelastic segment. Why cut price here?! Can we find some new innovation to add to the product which could justify getting the price back up to $18 again? Or, how about staying where we are on Blue TB but also introducing a Monarch Blue 79 to get some of the *price sensitive* business as well as the *quality sensitive* business? An evaluation of this option needs to take into consideration the fact that this approach might involve too much obfuscation of Monarch's basic fabric dyes strategy—the "Trubrite system."

Red dye also raises interesting cost-volume-profit (C-V-P) issues. Given the $10.30 contribution per pound, Monarch could certainly afford some price cutting if desired to hold volume. The real question is whether it is worth trying to buy away the Red 66 volume at a discount price. This is similar to the blue situation where it is important to keep the strategic positioning of the product in mind. Is Monarch competing on a price basis (a commodity) or on the basis of a differentiated product with higher quality and better service? One could argue, based on a C-V-P analysis of the data in Exhibit 3, that Red dye is a technological leader (with an exclusive patent) where the key to maintaining market share is superior value, not a cheaper price.

Thus, Monarch is in a much different position regarding the trade-offs across cost, price, penetration, and profitability for yellow, blue, and red dyes. The key point here is that an overall pricing strategy for yellow, blue, and red does not seem possible. Yellow is in a *totally* different strategic niche and red and blue face *somewhat* different competitive situations. The point to emphasize is that product strategy drives the pricing question. Consistent pricing is only possible when strategies are the same.

In terms of the following classic "pricing triangle" diagram, pricing for all three colors was value driven at the time of introduction of the new Trubrite system. By 1983, red was still value driven, but blue was C-V-P driven and yellow was competition driven. Intelligent cost analysis in 1983 must take these differences into account.

Which Leg Dominates in Setting Price

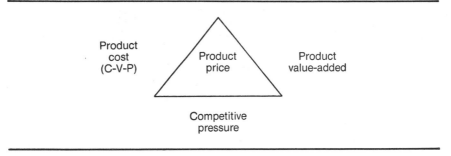

Strategically Differentiated Management Controls

At this point, we turn attention to the issue of differentiating management controls in accordance with the different strategic positions of the three Trubrite dyes.

Yellow Dye. There are three strategic keys here, given that Monarch does not and cannot have a differentiated product. The three are cost, cost, and cost. Monarch can only continue to compete aggressively on a price basis if they can reduce manufacturing costs. As shown in Table 7–1, cost savings *are* possible, depending on how aggressive one is about achievable cost targets.

In 1983, the company did introduce a program of new management controls in which a major element was cost reporting that focused on *theoretical* standards rather than currently achievable standards. The manager in charge of the yellow dye was tightly held against the theoretical standards. By showing theoretical standards and emphasizing where actual cost falls short of what is ideal, the hope is that managers will have a strong incentive not to settle for the currently achievable standard. If the regular reporting system focuses month by month on opportunities (perhaps impractical in the short run) for cost improvement, rather than burying these challenges as part of so-called attainable standards, more progress could be made toward realizing those opportunities. Does it really make sense, for example, to use high priced diluents (which were part of the original high value image) for yellow dye now that it is a cost driven commodity product? The pros and cons of such a switch should at least be discussed. This is a behavioral argument which we believe is sound and which Monarch is trying to implement. As an aside, we have also seen this same behavioral argument applied successfully in a major American steel company. This idea has proved successful in "real life" for Yellow Trubrite dye. By the end of 1983, the standard cost was down from $5.72 to $4.94. By 1984 it was down to $3.84 so that full cost profit

TABLE 7–1   Yellow TB Dye—Standard Cost Per Pound (as of 1982)

	Variable Cost	Share of Fixed Cost	Total Cost
Theoretical ideal	$2.18	$0.80	$2.98
Cost due to inefficient handling techniques	—	.32	3.30
Yield losses from non-ideal product formulation	.54	—	3.84
Loss from inefficient drying techniques	—	.56	4.40
Extra cost from use of higher priced diluents	.54	—	4.94
Loss from inefficient product flow manufacturing	—	.34	5.28
Cost premium from not using long-run supply contracts	.44	—	5.72
	$3.70	$2.02	$5.72*

*$5.72 is the "attainable" Standard Cost for 1982
Note: By focusing attention on the cost improvement opportunities through regular cost reporting of variances in the above format, the firm was able to achieve the following improvement in standard cost. Much of the improvement in fixed cost came from the factory modernization project.

1983—Standard Cost = $4.94
1984—Standard Cost = $3.84
1985—Standard Cost = $2.98

could be shown at a $4.20 price. By 1985 the standard cost was down to $2.98. The fixed cost savings were achieved largely through the plant modernization project. But the variable cost savings from diluents and long-term supply contracts involve policy issues. The innovative and aggressive posture toward cost control in internal financial reporting helped Monarch achieve cost savings which permitted it to reduce price again by 10 percent (to $3.82) in 1985 and still show a 20 percent net margin on sales. This led Trojan to exit the yellow dyes business altogether. This is a powerful strategic tool in those instances where cost leadership is critical. In terms of differentiated management controls, a key idea for yellow dye was clearly to focus on avenues for cost improvement via a reporting format such as Table 7–1.

Red and Blue Dye.   One could argue that the same cost reporting idea applies equally well to red or blue dye. We disagree because we think cost leadership thinking is inappropriate for high value added/highly differentiated products. Under this view, the strategic thrust for red and blue should be quality improvement, additional features, lots of service, and aggressive promotion of the product superiority, *not cost cutting*. For Red TB dye, the key issue is how to maintain product leadership. What investments can be made to prolong the leadership position of the product? A key management control would be reports focusing on product leadership variables. Milestone reporting on the development project for hot spray dyeing is much more critical for Red TB dye than is cost cutting. For blue dye the issue is niching versus penetration. *Smaller* may well be better, if margins can be maintained. A key management control for Blue TB dye thus is reporting focusing on cost-volume-profit relationships via comparative profit contribution totals.

Is cost cutting applicable to all three? Whereas it might well make sense to use lower priced "diluents" in the yellow dye to save 54 cents per pound with no noticeable drop in quality, such thinking would be off base for red or blue. For Monarch, cost for red and blue actually rose during 1983–85 while cost for yellow was dropping. This may not be bad news and it may not be accidental. One does not seriously consider putting plastic upholstery in a Mercedes Benz! Peters and Pascarella (1984) echo a similar view when they say: "There is not an institution in the world that has the capability to walk and chew gum simultaneously. The managerial pie is only 360 degrees, and if 348 of those degrees are aimed at paper-clip counting, you are not going to be paying attention to quality, service, and the next generation of products" (p. 61). Again, this is a behavioral assessment. Whether or not one agrees with their conclusion or with the management control implications, it does seem imperative to us that management control take explicit notice of the strategic context in which it is being applied.

In summary, cost analysis (for product profitability enhancement) and management control (to focus management attention on key success factors) are ideas that have been around for a long time. The point of this chapter is that the role of cost analysis and management control really depend on the strategy being followed and that smart cost analysis and control are differentiated, depending on strategy.

DISCUSSION QUESTIONS

1. What strategic cost analysis ideas can you identify based on the Trubrite case? Are they generalizable? To what types of business situations?
2. Can you identify other elements of management controls that could be differentiated in accordance with low cost versus differentiation strategies?
3. What are the best arguments you can make for *not* differentiating management controls across business units in a firm?

4. Do you believe the arguments for differentiating the controls are strong enough to offset your answer to Question 3?
5. Is your answer to Question 4 situational? If so, on what factors would the choice (differentiated controls or not) hinge?

REFERENCES

Kiechel, W. "The Decline of the Experience Curve." *Fortune*, October 5, 1981.

Peters, T., and P. Pascarella. "Searching for Excellence: The Winners Deliver on Value." *Industry Week,* April 16, 1984, pp. 61–62.

PART FOUR

Strategic Financial Analysis Which Isn't

CHAPTER 8

Strategic Financial Analysis for Long-Term Major Investments

In this chapter we present a case study which concerns the timberland holdings of a major paper and wood products company. Whether to retain a very large investment (4.6 million acres) or divest part or even all of it is the subject of the case. This is certainly a major strategic decision for the firm since it involves billion dollar cash flows spread out over 30- to 50-year growth cycles.

The case study is included in the book for two reasons. First, it illustrates very nicely how the role of financial analysis shrinks dramatically when the strategic issues become this major—thus the subtitle, strategic financial analysis which *isn't*! As this case illustrates, very nicely, for problems of this duration and magnitude, financial analysis tends not to be very strategically oriented and strategic analysis tends not to be very financially oriented.

A second reason for including this case is the way it illustrates how the choice of internal accounting and reporting systems can play a major role in shaping the way firms look at the strategic issues. The accounting reports definitely constitute a *lens* through which management views the current results of its past strategic commitments. When that lens most closely resembles a pair of rose colored glasses, the strategic assessment process is affected in ways management may not fully appreciate.

NATIONAL PAPER'S TIMBERLANDS: WHITHER AND WHENCE

In 1987 National Paper was one of the largest producers of printing and writing paper and one of the largest private landowners. National Paper owned or controlled 4.6 million acres of timberland throughout the United States, an area larger than Massachusetts and Rhode Island combined. The book value of this investment was $1 billion.

Paper mills and solid wood products mills generally complement each other in terms of the kind of raw material demanded. *Roundwood* sourcing to paper mills typically consists of poor quality, low valued, small size bolts (or logs) that cannot be profitably milled by saw mills or plywood mills. Mill waste (e.g., edgings, trim, slabs, and peeler cores) can be so readily chipped and processed into paper that sawmill waste is often the preferred source of raw material for paper mills. It is widely viewed that processing roundwood into paper is the least profitable use of the tree.

Beginning in 1983, following a dramatic drop in land and stumpage values (Exhibit 2) and an increased emphasis on white paper manufacturing, National began to seriously question the need for its extensive land holdings. In fact, about one million of the acres no longer serviced any National operations at all. Exhibit 1 is a recap of the largest American corporate landowners in 1984 and their paper capacity. James River Corporation is included as one firm following a zero timber ownership strategy. In spite of the massive holdings reflected in Exhibit 1, forest products firms control only 14 percent of the timberland in the United States (68.5

EXHIBIT 1   The Largest Corporate Owners of U.S. Timberland and Their Paper Making Capacities, 1984

Company	Millions of Acres		1984 Capacity (000 tons) Paper and Board
	Owned	Controlled	
Champion International	5.2	1.6	5,557
International Paper	6.4	0.4	3,760
Weyerhaeuser	6.0	0	2,890
National Paper	4.4	0.2	3,320
Georgia-Pacific	4.2	0.5	2,477
Boise Cascade	3.2	0.5	2,890
Great Northern Nekoosa	2.8	0.1	2,129
Crown Zellerbach*	1.7	0.3	1,834
Scott	1.8	0.1	1,690
Mead	1.7	0.1	2,564
Union Camp	1.6	0.1	2,148
Burlington Northern	1.5	0.0	0
Potlatch	1.4	0.0	0
Westvaco	1.3	0.0	1,872
James River Corporation	0.0	0.0	1,324

*Acquired by Sir James Goldsmith in 1985. He retained the timber holdings and sold the paper mills to James River Corporation.

EXHIBIT 2   Timber Prices

Part A   Timber Prices in Region 6 of U.S. National Forests
[1960-Quarter 1 through 1982-Quarter 4]
[Quarters 1 through 92]

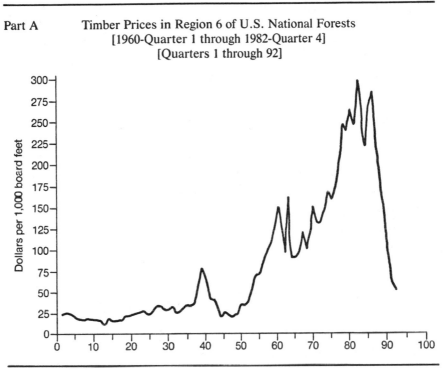

SOURCE: *Forest Science* 31, no. 2 (1985), p. 407.

Part B   Over a much longer time period, and stated in *real* prices,
the picture looks like this:

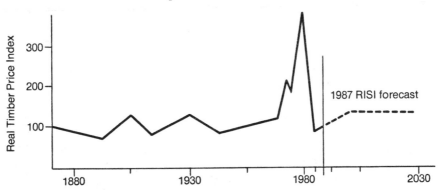

In short, real prices were at the same level in 1986 that they were in 1886. The
huge increase from 1973 to 1980 was followed by an even bigger decrease from
1980 to 1985.

million acres). The federal government controls 21 percent (102.4 million acres), other governmental units 6 percent, and miscellaneous private owners 58 percent (285.6 million acres). Even with 4.6 million acres, National typically supplies less than 50 percent of its fiber requirements from company land.

At the broadest level, there are four reasons for a paper and wood products company to own timber acreage:

1. Owned timber is an insurance policy to guarantee a source of supply for at least part of the basic raw material source. Fiber accounts for 15 to 25 percent of the manufacturing cost for a paper mill and a much larger percent for a lumber or plywood mill. The issue here is clearly a cost-benefit trade-off and a hedge against future uncertainty in raw material supply over the 30- to 50-year growing cycle.

2. Owned timber is a cash flow "smoothing" device. When demand is weak and cash flow is tight, a company with large timber holdings can use a higher than normal proportion of its own timber. This reduces corporate cash outflows since there is very little marginal outflow associated with harvesting trees that are mature.

3. Owned timber is a device to smooth reported earnings. When demand is weak, reported earnings are also lower than normal. Earnings can be increased by using a higher than normal proportion of owned timber which always shows a much lower cost than purchased timber. The book value of standing timber includes only the original planting costs. All annual upkeep costs are expensed as incurred. Thus, the book value of a mature stand of timber is almost always lower than the market price of the wood.

4. Timberland ownership can be viewed as a business of its own. The cash flows associated with ownership over the growing cycle would have to show an adequate rate of return on the invested capital, after allowing for the risks of the business, under this rationale for ownership.

It is interesting to note that the timing of when standing timber would be cut under this fourth rationale is the opposite of when it would be cut under the second and third rationales. As a business, timber would be cut when prices are strong (heavy demand) and would be allowed to stand when prices are weak (slack demand). As noted above, the second and third rationales involve cutting more timber when prices are weak and buying more timber (cutting less) when prices are strong.

As a general observation, it could be argued that National's cutting practices reflected the cash flow and earnings smoothing rationales to a large extent.

The Timberlands Division

The stated objectives of National's Timberlands operations were "to minimize the cost of wood supplied to company mills, to maximize the value obtained from timber harvested, to cost-effectively maximize the growth on company-controlled lands, and to assure that an adequate supply of wood fiber will be available at a favorable cost far into the future."

The Timberlands Division had been organized to coordinate National's southern forests in 1971 and had assumed nationwide responsibility in 1976. In addition to managing National's forests and harvesting from other lands under contract, Timberlands foresters were responsible for acquisition of all wood fiber for each mill. Thus, Timberlands people were located in each mill although their direct responsibility was to Timberlands headquarters.

Forestry

Forest users have long recognized that a forest can yield more than twice as much volume when efficiently and professionally managed. National used a wide range of activities to increase productivity on its lands. These included developing and planting genetically superior seedlings, thinning of stands to concentrate growth on the best trees, site preparation of the land before planting to eliminate competition from grasses and shrubs, pest and fire control, and fertilization of some lands deficient in essential nutrients. National conducted both a genetics improvement program and research into such areas as cloning and tissue cultures in order to continually improve the trees planted on its lands each year.

Timberlands management, as practiced by National and most other forest products firms, was similar to farming any other crop, with the major difference being the length of time between planting and harvest. These commercial forestry practices were decried by some as unnatural in that the result was far from being the typical "wild" forest. At harvest time, hunters and wildlife lovers complained that their sporting fields, enjoyed for decades, were being ruined.

Of course, one can also argue that cutting of mature trees is good for the forest because very old trees (like very old people) are much more susceptible to disease and pests that can then spread to younger trees as well. Essentially, forest management represents good *forestry* as well as good *business,* unless one believes that "benign neglect" is the right way to treat the forests.

The whole issue of managing corporate-owned forests, as well as government-owned forests, is as much emotional and political as it is financial. There are very few aspects on which it is really clear that the public interest diverges from the interests of the forest products companies. Even as apparently one-sided an issue as forest fires can be viewed two ways. The Forest Service until recently has regarded infestation and disease as nature's way but has not thought of fire similarly. Efforts to control forest fire have led to more intensive fires when they do occur. This has resulted in fires that completely devastate national forests and private ones as well, if they are in the way. In the typical fire in a healthy forest some trees will not be destroyed. For example, a healthy Ponderosa Pine has such a great resistance to fire that when the fire burns itself out, the Ponderosa Pine forms the core of the natural reforestation process. This is one reason the Ponderosa is so prevalent in the fire prone regions of the west and mountain states. But, when a forest is 'protected' from fire and becomes overly mature, even the Ponderosa will burn. This creates fires with much higher temperatures which will destroy even healthy trees. The Forest Service has recently begun to allow some fires to burn which, they now believe, will lead to more healthy and natural forests overall. But, can you really imagine Smokey the Bear saying, "Help stamp out *some* forest fires"?!!

Even claims in Maine about protecting the "wild" Allegash River from "desecration" conveniently ignore the fact that the Allegash basin was clear-cut by timber companies in the 1940s and 1950s. What stands there now as a wilderness has regrown naturally from bare stumps in about 40 years.

National is very interested in the way the national forests are managed since a large percentage of its supply of fiber comes from contract cuttings on national forest land. Overall, it just isn't clear what their future policies will be. Depending on what you read, the government may cut less timber, more timber, or just about the same amount as now.

National has nurseries in six states with capacity sufficient to fill virtually all the company's seedling needs, about 75 million in 1984—or about five for every tree that was harvested.

The Forestry Industry

The early forest products industry in the United States consisted primarily of mill operations that provided lumber and millwork for commerce and construction. In the late 19th century, most forest products companies practiced "cut and run" forestry. That is, they bought timber land in the lake states and the west, cut the best timber, and then allowed the land to revert to public ownership by failing to pay taxes. As the "timber barons" saw it, there was plenty of timber "out West" and there was little advantage in planting trees and waiting for them to mature. By 1900, with the forests of the northeast and the lake states stripped of the best virgin timber, the lumber industry shifted into the south and the Pacific northwest. In 1910, lumber production reached a peak of 40 billion board feet—a level that has been approached again only in recent years.

As the forests were cleared and the population increased, pressure mounted to curtail wasteful practices in the industry. The federal government responded by enacting the Organic Act of 1897, which carved forest reserves out of western federal lands. In 1905, these reserves became the basis for the National Forests system. Among other things, this act introduced "sustained yield" management based on the principle that the amount of timber harvested should not exceed the amount of timber grown. European countries had developed similar forestry practices a century before. It is worth noting that controlled cutting has always been a part of the national forests concept. It is really only the *relative* amount of cutting that generates so much controversy.

Long-term commitments to land ownership and good forestry were not widely adopted by private or corporate landowners until after World War II, because the returns to owners were not proportionate to the costs and risks involved in nurturing and holding timber over the long maturation period. Section 117(K) of the Internal Revenue Code of 1939 and its descendant, Section 631 of the Internal Revenue Code of 1954, were devised to provide a strong incentive to encourage practices that would ensure a permanent sufficient supply of timber. In essence, these sections of the IR Code allowed capital gains treatment for harvested timber and ordinary deductions for all operating costs as they are incurred, while only the direct costs of reforestation were capitalized. That is, after planting, all the annual expenses of forest management were expensed currently for tax purposes.

One result of these laws was that timber growing became a competitive investment opportunity. But not everyone takes advantage of the opportunity. In 1985, it was estimated that whereas 95 percent of corporately owned timberland was artificially regenerated, 85 percent of privately owned timberland was allowed to regenerate naturally. Of course, when *selective* cutting of mature trees from a forest is practiced, rather than *clear-cutting* the entire area, it is much less clear that planned replanting is necessary. Foresters clear cut because it isn't economically feasible to "hunt and pick" for certain trees once the loggers and trucks and equipment are on the site. Selective cutting is much less labor and capital intensive.

Mark Smith, vice president-controller of Forest Products, commented on several aspects of the Timberlands Division:

> The 1986 Tax Act is one more reason to question the long-term viability of the timberlands organization as it exists today. The lowering of tax rates and the elimination of special capital gains rates both serve to raise the after-tax cost of producing fee wood.

The question of how much land to own has always been difficult, with some companies relying on fee timberland almost completely and others buying all of their wood from outside sources. Reasons that we previously accepted for holding timberlands are now being questioned. Capital costs are high and the long-term profitability of holding timberlands is uncertain. *Recently,* some of the best financial performers in the paper industry are firms with little or no land. There is some question, however, whether their performance will be sustained. During the last few years, stumpage prices have been low relative to 1975 and there has been an abundant supply of wood. If prices begin to approach the 1975 levels again [Exhibit 2], wood costs will clearly have a dampening effect on the financial performance of those who buy all their wood.

The issue, as I see it, can be effectively summarized by the question: What is the effect on raw materials cost of various levels of fee timber backup? Almost any mill could be supplied completely from outside sources. However, the cost of doing this is to put ourselves at the mercy of the timber markets. During the late 1970s and early 80s, we saw declining wood supply and expectations of increased wood demand drive timber prices on West Coast government land up to a point where harvest was uneconomical [see Exhibit 2]. And this volatility is not only with West Coast timber. In the South, where a majority of our interests lie, pulpwood has long been described as being "in endless supply" and prices have increased only slowly and gradually. As recently as 1982, a government report indicated that growth was outstripping harvesting and that through the year 2030 there would be an ever-increasing supply of southern softwood. We now realize, however, that the government report was based on unrealistic data. A reevaluation of these data now indicates that removals to satisfy higher than forecast demand began to outpace growth in 1985. We expect this to continue so that by 2015, the total southern softwood growing stock will be in the neighborhood of 75 billion cubic feet rather than 150 billion cubic feet as earlier projected. Given higher demand and diminishing supply, timber prices should go up.

On the other hand, vast untapped timber resources exist outside of the United States, particularly in South America. In Brazil, where we have a mill and a 100,000 acre forest, we find that the Eucalyptus tree will regenerate three harvests from the same stump in a 25-year period. That is three times the growth rate from a fast-growing North American tree like the Loblolly Pine. The economics of that situation are pretty obvious. These developing countries, seeing wood prices rising in the United States, would be foolish not to develop their natural forest resources. And the economics favor developing their own conversion facilities, too. So we may be looking, at some point down the road, at significant new imports of pulp and paper products. This probably represents downward pressure on future domestic prices.

Rich Gates, general manager, Northeast Region, commented on the question, "Should National be in the forestry business?"

I suppose the purist would say, "If you have a better investment for your capital dollars, then sell Timberlands and invest the money elsewhere." This is all well and good, but what do you do with 4.6 million acres of land? You don't want to sell it at a loss. What's more, by selling the land and timber base, you may be selling one of the reasons why that alternative capital investment looks so good.

Let me explain. If we wanted to divest of all the Timberlands today, we would likely receive about $0.9 billion. The market for forest land in 1987 is pretty depressed. That amount of money could just about buy another mill. Assuming we do just that, how do we go about supplying this new mill at prices National is used to paying? The way I see it, three things could happen.

1. We could sell our lands to a competitor who can use all the excess wood in his own mill (effectively locking us out of a major source of wood),

2. We could sell to an investor with long term objectives and no need for immediate cash, or

3. We could sell to an investor with an interest in forest land and an immediate need for cash.

If the first or second occurs we can expect to pay more for our wood. In both cases, fiber would likely be withheld from our mill until the price increased appreciably from current levels. This could be as simple as holding timber for a winter harvest. How much increase? I don't know, it depends on the circumstances. If the increase were 30 percent and the current raw material cost to our mill accounts for 20 percent of all costs, then our finished product costs would increase 6 percent per ton. Certainly this would have a negative influence on our profitability.

If we sell to a third party who is in need of cash, we may not see any impact on wood supply. The third party will need to generate cash flow immediately. All we'd lose is the timber profits. But, we would incur substantial risk of higher wood costs in the future.

What I'm saying is that we have to study the situation at each location before we decide to sell timberlands in quantity. Timberlands now supplies low-cost wood to our mills. Our land ownership position also tends to depress local market price. How? When the cost of outside wood increases, we cut more of our own wood and buy less which tends to drive the outside price back down again.

Do we need 4.6 million acres of land? No. However, let's be careful about *where* we divest. There are "hidden" benefits in timberland ownership that are not apparent in the marketplace until they are gone.

Bill Boone, general manager, Southern Region, commented on the impact of his region's land base on National's mills.

If we sold our Texas land base to a third party we probably would not see much impact on our paper mills. Prices may rise a little, but all in all, we should be able to supply them. After all, the buyer of our land will also want to sell wood to recover his investment.

This would not necessarily be true for our plywood mills. I see no way to supply those mills and operate them profitably without a land base. There is a real question about the total wood supply. When supply is constrained, prices rise. The recent purchase of the Kirby tract (previously owned by the Santa Fe Railroad) by Louisiana Pacific demonstrates this. LP has a different management philosophy than we do. They have curtailed clear cutting and now practice selective cutting. As a consequence, they have reduced the supply of wood from their lands and are relying more on the open market. Stumpage has increased from around $100–$120 per 1,000 board feet to about $150 since last November and is expected to escalate further. At this point there is no end in sight. It will likely stabilize somewhere near the break-even value of the wood we can cut from the log. We will need a real increase in current building products prices to prevent declining profits from our wood products operations.

And, if we sold or closed plywood mills, we would have to break our very profitable contracts to supply wood chips to our paper mill in Texas.

The task of justifying Timberlands ownership is a difficult one, I know. The direct profits of Timberlands operations, mineral leases, and recreational leases are easily quantifiable, but they are only a portion of the benefits derived from Timberlands ownership. How do we quantify the benefit of price stability to our mills? What value should we assign to the stable supply of raw material? What's the risk of temporary shutdowns caused by seasonal shifts in the open market wood supply, and what is the resultant cost? What is an acceptable risk?

These questions should be addressed separately for each region. Perhaps they should be asked at a level below the region, that is, for individual tracts of land. If the return from the sale of the land is greater than the risks associated with not owning the land, maybe those tracts should be sold or traded.

Financial Considerations

The economic returns from the timber business are extremely difficult to measure because they involve cash flows spread over very long periods of years and widely differing beliefs about the future. One component in the calculation is the trend in prices for the land upon which the timber grows. Over the period from 1950 to 1983 timberland prices, excluding timber, grew at a compound 9 percent rate in a 34 state survey. Prices were generally depressed from 1982 through 1986. Future price trends are the subject of much highly diverse speculation. *Fortune* reported in June, 1985 that American Can was struggling to get rid of .5 million acres which is valued at $220 million ($440/acre). American Can believed that pension funds were likely to invest $1 billion in timberlands over the next five years. *Pension World* confirmed the interest in timberlands in a March 1986 story which cited a John Hancock study showing timber investment returns of 10.5 percent compounded between 1958 and 1984 (versus common stocks at 9.6 percent). *Business Week,* in February 1985, cited a U.S. Forest Service estimate that timberland would increase in value 2.1 percent a year faster than inflation over the next 45 years. In 1985, *Pension World* cited Equitable Insurance as believing timberland to be as great a current investment opportunity as commercial real estate had been in the 1970s.

On the other hand, 7 to 10 million acres of timberland was "on the market" in 1987 with very few large-scale buyers. Prime tracts were selling for 30 to 50 percent below appraised value. A widely cited study by the University of Georgia School of Forestry showed that southern pine pulpwood had actually declined in real value between 1952 and 1982. DRI forecasts in 1985 indicated flat real timberland prices over the following 20 years, but these forecasts were widely criticized in the industry. A Mead Corporation study described in *Pulp and Paper* in July 1985 indicated internal rates of return on timber investments ranging only between 10 percent and 14 percent which, at best, barely meet the cost of capital. The Mead study was also bearish on timber investment because of extreme uncertainty about future global supply/demand patterns, the relative illiquidity of the investments, and the reduced attractiveness of such projects under the new tax proposals (which are now in effect).

Forbes (December 1985) saw well-managed long-term investments in timber earning 4 to 6 percent above inflation, but *Fortune* (June 1985) cited security analysts who felt that timberland was substantially overpriced, even at the relatively depressed levels ($250 to $350 per acre) based on recent past history. One interesting piece of evidence often cited is the purchase by Sir James Goldsmith of Crown Zellerbach in 1985. He promptly sold the paper mills to James River, keeping only the timberland and some miscellaneous assets. The acquisition of 1.7 million acres (and cutting rights to another .3 million acres) by such an internationally acclaimed investor seems to be a major vote of confidence for the timberland business. However, of the $570 million he invested, Goldsmith recouped $400 million from selling the non-timber holdings. He thus acquired the timberland for only about $100 per acre. In April of 1985, CZ had estimated that the timberland was worth $500 per acre. Buying it for $100 per acre is more easily viewed as a steal than a commitment to the business.

John Baxter, vice president of Timberlands Operations, commented on the past financial performance of Timberlands and offered some potential strategies for the future.

> During the decade immediately preceding 1984, Timberlands was a major contributor to profits and cash flow. It contributed nearly $1 billion in cash flow from a 3 million acre land base. This equated to a $333 return per acre

from a land base whose invested capital value averaged about $140/acre. We returned well over twice the land's book value in cash flow during the decade; this amounted to average annual return of 24 percent on invested capital.

This excellent performance was not achieved without a cost to the corporation. Lands that were supposed to supply 50 percent of the resource demand were used to supply between 70 and 100 percent depending on the Region. The result of these high harvest levels of the past is that fewer acres will be available for harvest during the next two decades.

Recognizing the impact of reduced future harvest activity on Timberlands performance, the entire Division was reorganized in 1986. Salaried positions were reduced by 21 percent. Logging and site preparation crews were eliminated in favor of outside contractors. In total, head count, both salaried and hourly, was reduced by nearly 60 percent.

Following the reorganization we completed a fairly thorough study that was designed to estimate the long-term contribution of the controlled land base to National's profits and cash flow. [The results of this analysis are presented in Exhibit 3.] It should not be too difficult to see the impact of the reduced harvest over the next two decades. Profits and cash flow are expected to decline by nearly one fourth, as is return on capital employed. These forecasts certainly don't paint a rosy picture for the Division.

Given the benefit of 20/20 hindsight, would we still have cut as aggressively as we did during the last decade? Probably yes. In answering that question we have to consider the past goals of the corporation. National was in the midst of a fairly heavy capital investment program. Cash was urgently needed to support the building of two new paper mills. Monetization of our timber resource seemed to be an effective way to generate dollars for capital spending without incurring major debt. Besides, we didn't mistreat our lands. The lands that were harvested were reforested and are currently in optimum growth production.

We in Timberlands are not naive. We recognize that we cannot justify a corporate commitment to forestry that is based on past performance. We need to review our land management programs as business enterprises and aggressively seek ways to improve our financial performance. Based on current thinking, we see many opportunities to improve the financial performance of our land management program. Among them are:

1. Identify and market tracts of land that have higher value under alternative use. Some of these alternative uses include residential (both rural and semirural), commercial, recreational, and agricultural development. We see very real opportunities developing in Florida, East Texas, Eastern and Western North Carolina, New York, New Hampshire, Vermont, and Maine. We think that we can, over a 10-year-period, profitably sell about 110,000 acres in this manner.

2. Reduce wood costs by either (a) trading lands with other owners to achieve a better spatial distribution of the land base or (b) buy and sell wood locally. Both approaches will reduce wood cost by reducing transportation costs.

EXHIBIT 3

TIMBERLANDS EVALUATION SYSTEM (T.E.S.)
Profit and Loss Statement*
(in thousands of dollars)

Division totals
gross acres = 6,347,462

Period	Revenue	Wood-cost	Exp. Roads	Svrnc Prpty Tax Prtctn	Depre-ciation	Over-head	Profit
1986–1990	213,446	165,551	6,293	10,851	3,126	27,456	101,540
1991–1995	256,321	133,101	5,469	10,589	3,406	25,108	78,648
1996–2000	255,650	127,421	5,477	10,626	3,158	25,417	83,551
2001–2005	260,022	124,738	5,703	10,791	2,639	26,439	89,712
2006–2010	328,703	154,484	5,880	10,996	2,228	27,668	127,447
2011–2015	403,825	190,296	5,915	11,170	1,989	27,682	166,793
2016–2020	447,938	204,393	6,174	11,467	1,912	28,081	195,911
2021–2025	412,723	189,638	6,322	11,632	1,854	28,003	175,274
2026–2030	395,577	187,930	6,415	11,453	1,637	23,702	164,440
2031–2035	505,504	254,482	6,424	12,100	1,515	23,682	207,301

*Real dollars, assuming RISI stumpage escalation—annual averages within 5-year period.

EXHIBIT 3 (concluded)

Period	Present Value	Capital	Capital Lease Pmts	Cash Flow	Return on Sales	Return on Book	Return on Capital Employed
1986–1990	90,003	22,106	5,065	91,516	32.3	16.9	14.4
1991–1995	52,369	13,769	5,065	75,723	30.7	12.5	10.8
1996–2000	41,744	12,201	5,065	80,070	32.7	12.8	11.2
2001–2005	33,429	11,531	5,065	86,418	34.5	13.3	11.7
2006–2010	35,487	12,079	5,065	125,123	38.8	18.5	16.4
2011–2015	34,705	14,037	5,065	167,547	41.3	24.1	21.4
2016–2020	30,461	14,457	5,065	198,085	43.7	28.6	25.4
2021–2025	20,364	13,114	5,065	176,834	42.5	25.9	23.0
2026–2030	14,277	12,423	0	164,275	41.6	24.3	21.6
2031–2035	13,449	15,081	0	207,111	41.0	30.6	27.2

Cumulative present value = 1,831,450

Cumulative cash flow = 6,863,509

3. Expand our hunting and recreational lease programs to generate more cash return from the lands each year.

4. Invest in manufacturing facilities in places where specific opportunities exist to monetize particular forest properties at an attractive return to the corporation.

We are only now beginning to seriously investigate these and other opportunities.

In considering the Timberlands question, Matt Clemens, chairman and CEO, observed:

We are looking at several complex issues that interact in ways that make rational, systematic analysis very difficult. First, we want to become the leading white paper company in the world. White paper is the segment with the highest profits and the greatest growth potential—a doubling of domestic demand is projected over the next 50 years. In the international arena, even greater growth is anticipated. Also, there are fewer substitutes for white paper than other grades. For example, you might think of sending a package in a plastic, rather than manila, envelope. But you wouldn't publish *National Geographic* on anything but Kromekote. Further, the white paper business has not experienced the demand and price volatility of other segments of the forest products business.

Given that this is where National wants to be, what should be our position regarding Timberlands? Have we really been involved in forestry just because of the tax breaks? If we were to simply harvest what we have already planted and sell the land after harvest we would eventually become totally dependent on outside sources for our most important raw material. Would it be available in 50 years? At what prices? And, if we continue to operate Timberlands, will the economics of operating under the new tax laws allow us to produce at a reasonable profit and still effectively compete with foreign paper firms? Should we sell our timberlands? If we do and if the government later revises taxes to restore the incentives for forestlands, it may not be possible to recreate this level of resources—the forests, the silvicultural researchers, the skilled foresters—again.

Finally, how should I evaluate these trade-offs with regard to National's current responsibility to its stockholders and its responsibility to future managers and future generations of Americans? While I plan to hold this job for a while longer, I know that the operational effects of a decision in this area will not be noticed for years or even decades after I'm gone.

The basic economics of the forestry business in 1987 are illustrated in the following table which summarizes selected facts from three regions of the country in which National has major timber holdings:

	For 1 Acre of Timberland		
	Texas	Maine*	Washington
Growing cycle	30 years	50 years	50 years
Current site preparation cost	$ 62	$ 12	$ 95
Planting cost	44	0	130
Forest management cost/year†	5	2	9
Ad valorem tax/year	3	1	2
Total cost in year 0 (not deductible until sale)	106	12	225
Total annual cost over the growing cycle (fully tax deductible)	8	3	11
Current revenue yield (weighted average of pulpwood and sawtimber yield)	924	195	4,150
Estimated market value of the land, *ex* trees	200	100	300

*Maine timberland is allowed to regenerate naturally.

†Annual forest management expenses include road construction and maintenance, silviculture, fire control, boundary maintenance, inventory costs, and division overhead.

Assignment Questions

1. Using the information in the table at the end of the case, evaluate the prospective profitability over the growing cycle of planting one acre of trees in Texas, Maine, and Washington. The time value of money is obviously one issue here since the cash flows are spread over many years. Present your analysis in *real* terms in order to eliminate one major assumption (future inflation rates). You may also assume that land values for timberland (*ex* trees) will move in direct proportion to timber or "stumpage" prices. Use a tax rate of 35%.

   Do you believe it is more useful to make assumptions about real price escalation and solve for an expected rate of return or to assume a break-even real hurdle rate and solve for the implicit price escalation necessary to yield that return?

   Can you think of some way to structure the economic analysis other than ROI for an assumed price escalation or the implicit price escalation rate necessary for an assumed ROI?

2. Try to summarize the arguments supporting National's current position as an owner of 4.6 million acres of timberland.

3. Critique these arguments, considering strategic issues as well as financial returns.

4. Evaluate the following quotation (1986) from James Samartini, vice president for financial resources, Mead Corporation: "Timberlands are no longer a strategic asset, they are a financial asset and increasingly need to be managed as such."
5. What do you believe should be National's timberlands strategy in 1987? Why?

NATIONAL PAPER TIMBERLANDS—A COMMENTARY

The National Paper Timberlands case is a very rich and complex one which we use at Tuck as the last class in a 24-session course called Managerial Accounting. There is sufficient financial information in the case to permit students to virtually bury themselves in numbers if they want to view the case as an exercise in financial analysis. There is a certain surface plausibility to the notion that National would only be in the tree business if they believe, ex ante, that the expected returns are good. Thus, since they *are* in the business in a very big way, it should be possible to show reasonable returns, somehow, based on case facts.

And, on the surface, case Exhibit 3 seems to suggest that the business shows positive present value over a 50-year horizon when the cash flows are discounted at some unspecified but presumably reasonable real discount rate. However, Exhibit 3 is a snake pit for those who try to tackle it rationally! This is a *live* exhibit given to me by the vice president for Timber Operations, in the presence of the controller of Timber Operations. Yet neither I nor anyone else who has ever studied it carefully can figure out what is going on! Suffice it to say that there are sufficient readily apparent inconsistencies and contradictions in the exhibit to make it clear to anyone who studies it even casually that one cannot get to the conclusion (positive present value over 50 years) from the numbers presented. But, it is also true that the senior management of the Timberlands division all believe the conclusion. When pressed about the exhibit, they almost uniformly argue that there *must* be some plausible but unspecified explanation for the apparent inconsistencies—something has just been left out of the table, they say.

When the students try to answer question one, they also discover some serious problems. Table 8–1 shows the cash flows for each of the three examples along with the estimated IRRs. This table also shows the implicit compound growth rate in real land and timber prices necessary to yield a 15 percent real ROI.

The table shows that using the "best available" forecast (RISI) of real price growth, the economic returns are dismal! One must assume extremely high rates of real price increase to show reasonable rates of return. It is true that timber prices increased at about 10 percent, com-

TABLE 8–1

After-Tax Cash Flows and IRRs
Assume 1 Percent Compound Real Escalation in Stumpage and Land
Values from 1987–2037 (the RISI forecast)

	$(1.01)^{30} = 1.35$	$(1.01)^{50} = 1.645$	
	Texas	*Maine*	*Washington*
Time 0	(200)	(100)	(300)
	(106)	(12)	(225)
	(306)	(112)	(525)
Years 1–30			
	(5.2)	(1.95)	(7.2)
Year 30	$924 \times 1.35 = \$1{,}247$		
	$200 \times 1.35 = \$270$		
	$\$1{,}247 - \$106 = $ Gain, $\$1{,}148$		
	Tax at 35% = \$399		
	$\$270 - \$200 = $ Gain, \$70		
	Tax at 35% = \$25		
	Total A/T inflow = \$1,093		
Years 31–50		(1.95)	(7.2)
Year 50	$\$195 \times 1.645 = \$321$	$\$4{,}150 \times 1.645 = \$6{,}827$	
	$\$100 \times 1.645 = \$165$	$\$300 \times 1.645 = \$494$	
	$\$321 - \$12 = \$309$	$\$6{,}827 - \$225 = \$6{,}602$	
	$\$309 \times .35 = \$108$	$\$6{,}602 \times .35 = \$2{,}311$	
	$\$165 - \$100 = \$65$	$\$494 - \$300 = \$194$	
	$\$65 \times .35 = \$23$	$\$194 \times .35 = \$68$	
	Total A/T inflow = \$355	Total A/T inflow = \$4,942	
IRR	3.3%	1.3%	4.0%
Rate of real price escalation needed to yield 15% IRR	12+%	14+%	11+%

pounded between 1950 and 1983 or between 1958 and 1984, but start and stop dates are critical here. Prices rose phenomenally from 1973 to 1979 and dropped even more phenomenally from 1980 to 1986. From 1956 to 1986 real prices actually fell. So, what is a reasonable forecast of future prices? It becomes very difficult to see any plausible prospect of a reasonable return on the invested capital unless one is very pessimistic about future timber supply relative to demand.

Herein lies the "Catch 22" of the analysis. For any given scenario of timber demand, if one is optimistic about future timber supply, the implication is weaker future timber prices. But, then the implied rate of return to those who supply the timber is not very good. But, if the expected return is not very good, there is no reason to make the investment now. This implies reduced future supply of timber. If the future supply is reduced, future timber prices will be higher. Then, if one projects higher future prices there should be more investment in trees now. But more investment now yields more future supply which hurts future prices. And so on.

This is a clear example of the *contrarian investment paradox*. When many people believe something is a good investment, the fact that they do all invest will make the investment a bad one for all of them. If many people believe something is a bad investment, the fact that many do not invest will make the investment a good one for the few who do. That is, for a situation like this one, the only way to earn superior returns is to bet *against* the crowd. If one assumes that the crowd in this case is a reasonably intelligent group (senior management of America's leading paper companies), it becomes clear that betting against the crowd is a risky proposition. This, of course, is exactly what investment theory would suggest—the only way to earn above average returns is to take above average risks.

James River Corporation's strategy of not investing in timberlands should thus be profitable for them as long as most major forest products firms do invest. Conversely, National's strategy of investing heavily in timberlands is only likely to be profitable for them if many major firms do not. One inference from this contrarian paradox is that formal financial analysis is essentially irrelevant for major, long-run investments like this. The prevalent assumptions about future prices (predicated on future supply) are self-defeating! Thus, trying to marshall the "best current thinking" about future trends is only useful to the extent one then acts in contradition to the "experts"! For decisions of this magnitude and duration, strategic analysis is thus essentially devoid of much conventional financial analysis. That is the first major point of the case.

The narrative in the case is very revealing of the kinds of responses people often offer when they feel very strongly about something but cannot muster much objective evidence in support of it. I am cynical about most of the arguments presented in the case because I don't believe they can withstand much careful attention. But, I'm glad the shoe is not on my foot trying to explain rationally why the Tuck MBA program should not be closed immediately as a useless waste of the students' time and money. MBA education in 1987 is very probably just as subject to the contrarian paradox as is tree farming!

For the record, let's review the arguments in support of continued heavy forestry investment by National that are presented in the case. Both Rich Gates and Bill Boone stress the impact of National's ownership on the level and stability of wood prices paid by National's mills. Gates makes the argument for pulpwood and Boone makes it for plywood "peeler" logs, but their conclusions are the same—National Mills pay lower and more stable prices over time when National is a major wood supplier. John Baxter, on the other hand, cites Timberlands' major contribution to corporate earnings and cash flow, at a very favorable rate of return on capital employed, during the decade of 1973 to 1983. The skeptic in me wants to point out that this decade of Timberlands' prosperity (1973–1983) cited by Baxter was hardly one of low and stable wood prices. If the goal is low and stable prices at the mill, 1973–1983 was a disastrous decade! But, when prices are stable at low levels, the profitability of the Timberlands' investment suffers. You really can't have it both ways.

When one views wood prices from the perspective of a mill manager, low and stable prices are clearly a great boon. Gates and Boone are very close to this perspective. But what is the cost of achieving this target? If we assume that Gates is correct about the market value of the aggregate timberland holdings (say $0.9 billion versus book value of $1.4 billion), National could realize $1.1 billion in cash by the sale (assuming a 40 percent tax rate). If this money were used to retire debt (12 percent deductible cost) and equity (15 percent after-tax cost) in a one-third, two-thirds ratio (the target capitalization ratio for the firm), the impact on profit before taxes would be a saving of $227 million each year ($366 million × 12% + $734 million × 15%/.6 = $44 million + $183 million). From Exhibit 3 in the case, we know that the market value of internal timber purchases was running at about $214 million in 1986 (the transfer price between Timberlands and the mills is estimated current market price). Thus, prices would have to rise on average by about 106 percent (227/214) before the trade-off was unfavorable! Even the 30 percent rise in wood prices mentioned *negatively* by Gates would actually constitute a very *favorable* trade-off for National.

It is true that selling the Timberlands means assuming new risks regarding future wood prices. But when one probes the magnitude of the prospective price increases which would be necessary to offset the cost of carrying the investment, the risk seems much less clear. This suggests that Baxter's is the stronger argument—Timberlands is a good investment because, over time, wood transfer prices (market prices) exceed the costs of planting and growing the trees by enough to show a good return on the invested capital. And it is clearly true, according to case Exhibit 3, that Timberlands always shows a very good return on sales and return on invested capital over the years. This would have been particularly true in the decade from 1973 to 1983.

Herein lies the second major element of the richness of the case. It is true that Timberlands almost always (year after year after year) shows very good results in the financial statements of National. But it is also true that the financial statements totally misconstrue the true financial situation, even over long enough periods to encompass complete growth cycles. We often tell our students that *over the long run* financial statements cannot lie. Accounting conventions that inflate or penalize short-run earnings eventually even out. In the long run, profit equals "cash *in*" minus "cash *out*" and accounting conventions cannot camouflage this relationship for a steady state business forever. Because this piece of wisdom is so sound, virtually all of the time, we can be lulled into thinking it always holds. The tree business is thus a shock to accountants when they realize that the financial statements can lie year after year after year.

To see the lie, we need only construct a simple example and follow the accounting over the years:

Assume:
1. A 30-year growth cycle for trees.
2. Each year for 30 years we buy one acre and plant it in trees.
3. After 30 years, each year we cut one acre and replant it.
4. It costs $100 to buy one acre, $100 to plant one acre of trees, and $10 per acre per year in forest management expenses. Assume no escalation in these costs.
5. An acre of mature timber can be sold for $2,500. Assume no change in this price over the years.

The annual cash flows for this example can readily be calculated as follows:

Year 1	(210)
Year 2	(220)
⋮	
Year 20	(400)
⋮	
Year 30	(500)
	2,500
Year 31	(400) *steady state* forever
	2,500
⋮	

Once the steady state is reached, the accounting results are also readily calculated:

Assets (30 acres at $200 each)	$6,000 *every year*
Revenues (sale of one acre of timber)	$2,500 *every year*
Expenses ($100 planting cost from 30 years ago for the acre harvested this year and $10/acre/year times 30 acres for upkeep expenditures *this* year)	$ 400 *every year*

This follows the accounting conventions used by virtually every forest products firm in America: capitalize land cost and planting cost as inventory; expense all annual upkeep expenditures as incurred.

Thus, each year the firm will show $2,100 of profit ($2,500 − $400), a return on sales of 84 percent (2,100/2,500) and a return on assets of 35 percent (2,100/6,000). Even on a before-tax basis, these are very healthy returns—well above average for American industry. Even with a one-third tax rate, the after-tax return on assets is over 23 percent (1,400/6,000). Yet, these reported results are a lie! Would one be foolish to trade this business for one earning "only" 10 percent return on assets? The answer is no! In fact, this business is earning only 6 percent real return each year. This fact can be readily verified as follows:

Cash Flows over the Full 30-Year Cycle for Any One Acre

	Before Tax	After Tax	
Year 0	(200)	(200)	
Years 1–30	(10)	(6.67)	
Year 30	2,500	1,700	($2,500 − $100 = Gain, $2,400 Tax = ⅓ × $2,400 = $800)
	100	100*	

Note: 30-year IRR = 6.0%
*Assume the acre is sold at the end of the cycle to get a true return over the full cycle.

Thus, year after year, each and every acre of timber earns exactly 6.0 percent (after tax) over its growth cycle. Yet, miraculously, year after year, the acre harvested shows an accounting return of 23 + percent (after tax) on assets employed. Who says there is no free lunch?! This lie never self-corrects—it stays a lie year after year into perpetuity.

Once the trees have been harvested from an acre, the question of whether or not it makes more sense to replant again or to sell the acre is clearly very complex and difficult. It depends upon 30-year forecasts of wood supply and wood demand and annual upkeep expenses. The replanting decision also depends upon one's tolerance for risk of price fluctuations and supply fluctuations. It is clear that in order to earn a reasonable economic return, one must assume substantial escalation in future timber prices. Thus, as an investment, planting trees is very much a play on future price escalation. In the example here, the return without escalation is only 6 percent. It can be readily calculated for this example that compound price escalation of 4 percent is required to earn an economic return of 10 percent. It is thus also clear that the higher the price escalation, the higher the rate of return. It is an historical fact that from 1886 to 1986 there was virtually no escalation in real timber prices. But, from 1974 to 1980 there was a phenomenal leap in prices. This was followed between 1980 and 1985 by an even more phenomenal fall in prices. What to forecast for the next 30 years is a very open question made even more complex by the contrarian paradox described above.

One other thing is clear about timber profitability—generally accepted accounting principles grossly overstate the profitability of trees that are now being cut because GAAP ignores the time value of the money tied up over the growing cycle. This is *not* a problem in forecasting because the cash flow stream for trees now being cut is an historical fact as is the past pattern of interest rates. No guessing or forecasting is necessary to calculate the ex post earned return over the just completed growing cycle. Conventional accounting *could* report this profit accurately but it *does not*. All that is required is to allow for implicit interest on the money which was tied up during the growth cycle.

To illustrate how the accounting could work if management chose to tell the truth instead of a lie, we can use the same example with one additional assumed fact. Assume that the cost of money over the 30-year growth cycle is a constant 12 percent per year.[1] Note that for any given

---

[1]This is a conservative pre-tax equivalent of a *real* after-tax weighted average cost of capital. With 3 percent real interest rates and one-third tax rate, the real after-tax cost of debt would be 2 percent. With a 12 percent after-tax real cost of equity, and a one-third, two-thirds ratio of debt and equity in the capital structure, the weighted average after-tax real cost of capital would be 8 ⅔ percent. This is 13 percent on a pre-tax equivalent basis.

firm and for any given past growth cycle, actual interest rates are a known fact. Now, in the year of sale, we can use the Residual Income concept to calculate realized profit as follows:

Sales	$ 2,500	
Cost of goods sold:		
Original planting cost	$(2,996)	[100 × (1.12)^{30}]
30 years of upkeep cost	$(2,704)	($10/year compounded at 12% for 30 years)
Loss	$(3,200)	

This kind of financial reporting is not only true, it is also totally practical because, at cutting time, all the 30-year cash flows and the interest rates in each of those years are known with certainty. Why do you suppose not one major forest products company uses this approach for its internal accounting reports?

We believe it is clear that the prevailing mindset in this country in the forest products companies is to always replant when you cut and to always manage your forests diligently. The very real uncertainty about the future of the business is nearly always resolved by almost all the companies in favor of continuing to invest rather than not to invest. Is this optimism about the future influenced by the fact that the tree business always looks very good in the accounting reports, year by year? Does the continuing *illusion* of 23 percent ROA (in the example here) delude management into an overly optimistic view about the uncertain future, encouraging a *false* sense of optimism? We believe the answers to these questions could well be *yes*.

Would *true* accounting for past timber investment decisions encourage a different view of the admittedly uncertain future prospects for current replanting decisions? In the example presented here, if management was seeing reports each year showing steady $3,200 annual losses from past investment decisions (a *true fact*), would this affect their attitude about continuing to invest? Might not *true* accounting for past losses serve as a useful counterpoint to the very understandable unbridled enthusiasm for "making new trees" which stirs in the bosom of every red-blooded forester, forestry researcher, and seasoned timberlands executive? We believe the answers to these questions also could well be *yes*.

Is it plausible that forest products companies would consciously choose to use untrue accounting reports so as not to be forced to confront unpleasant past realities while contemplating uncertain future possibilities about tree business economics? We believe that the answer to this question is very probably *no*. We believe in this situation, that self-delusion is more plausible than conscious deceit. It is entirely possible that forest industry managements actually believe the lie told by their accounting reports! In the case, John Baxter, who is a very intelligent, thoughtful, and successful senior executive certainly seems to believe it.

To understand why the executive management group at National is so reluctant to change the current Timberlands strategy, consider the following simplified 2x2 "payoff" table:

Possible Outcomes

	Timber Prices over the Next 40 Years	
	Rise Enough to Make the Ownership ROI Good	*Do Not Rise Enough to Make the ROI Good*
Sell the Timberlands	• Much current anxiety. • High level of perceived supply risk. • Lose the good apparent accounting returns. • Make a *bad* financial decision whose *real* results will only show up in the long run long after current management is gone.	• Much current anxiety. • High level of perceived supply risk. • Lose the good apparent accounting returns. • Make a *good* financial decision whose *real* results will only show up long term long after current management is gone.
Keep the Timberlands	• Avoid anxiety about major change. • Avoid perceived supply risk. • Keep the good apparent accounting returns. • Make a *good* financial decision whose *real* results will only show up in the long run long after current management is gone.	• Avoid anxiety about major change. • Avoid perceived supply risk. • Keep the good apparent accounting returns. • Make a *bad* financial decision whose *real* results will only show up in the long term after current management is gone.

Is it really so surprising that management stays with the status quo?

Accounting reports, to the extent possible, should be constructed to serve as a useful benchmark in thinking about future actions. Forest products companies clearly face a major set of strategic issues and strategic decisions regarding investment in the timber resource. Whether timber is *the* principal strategic resource for such firms or merely the primary raw material source, timber investment is big business for them. And strategic timber investment decisions clearly involve a horribly complex and uncertain future made even more difficult by the "contrarian paradox." Accounting for the past events is always a very subjective and uncertain process in real companies. "Truth" in accounting is very elusive. But, when firms use accounting reports that are demonstrably inaccurate while failing to use reports that would much more accurately reflect past decisions, they are unnecessarily limiting (and even misconstruing) the information available to them in analyzing their strategic options.

That really is the second central point of this commentary. Good strategic analysis deserves the best possible accounting support. Current practices in timberland accounting are, in our opinion, inexcusably inept in this regard because they totally ignore the unescapable reality of time value of money. The false favorable signals conveyed about the real profitability of past investments could well be a major factor in explaining the continuing optimism in the industry in spite of very meager prospective financial returns. We see no reason to believe that the ineptitude is deliberate. Rather, we infer that the situation is perhaps the best example, of which we are aware, of the self-delusion which is possible when accounting is blithely accepted at face value.

We will close this commentary with what to us is a very interesting observation. When we use this case with MBA students, most of the class time is spent with financial analysis of one sort or another. The MBA students cannot believe that management would keep the investment if the numbers really look so bad. When we use this case in a program for National senior managers, most of the class time is spent discussing the risks and penalties for putting the company at the mercy of outside timber suppliers. The National managers cannot believe that someone would seriously try to reduce this uncertainty to a financial calculation.

DISCUSSION QUESTIONS

1. Try to summarize the arguments supporting National's current position as an owner of 4.6 million acres of timberland.
2. Critique these arguments, considering strategic as well as financial returns.

3. What can you learn about the role of financial analysis in such decisions? Are these lessons transferable? To what types of business decisions?
4. Do you believe that it is appropriate for GAAP to ignore the time value of money for forest products companies?
5. Why do you suppose all the major forest product firms ignore time value of money (the residual income concept) in their internal accounting reports?
6. What do you see as the generic elements of a decision for which financial analysis is not very useful?

Index